CW00708854

A GUIDE ⸰
THE HISTORIC
PARKS & GARDENS
OF TYNE AND WEAR

Researched and Compiled by

Fiona Green
on behalf of
Tyne and Wear Specialist Conservation Team

with

John Pendlebury
Gateshead Metropolitan Borough Council

&

Peter Jubb
City of Newcastle upon Tyne

Design by George Tullin
Cover by Steve Urwin

Published by the Tyne and Wear Specialist Conservation Team, Development Department, Newcastle upon Tyne City Council in association with Gateshead Metropolitan Borough Council, North Tyneside Council, Borough of South Tyneside and the City of Sunderland.

1995

ISBN 1 85795 086 0

INTRODUCTION

Landscape design has been called Britain's greatest contribution to European culture. Since the Garden History Society was formed in 1965 interest in garden heritage has grown substantially. The importance of this heritage was recognised in 1983 with the legislation which paved the way for the English Heritage Register of Parks and Gardens of Special Historic Interest. This Register gives statutory recognition to this very special legacy. At the time of writing there are 9 sites in Tyne and Wear included in the Register (denoted by a ^ in the guide) though it is likely that this will increase in the near future. It is hoped the guide will show that in addition to these sites of recognised national importance there are many other parks and gardens in the county of historic importance which deserve to be treasured. The guide does not pretend to give a comprehensive compilation of the county's rich landscape, but does provide representative examples of the major types of designed landscape and outlines the influences which lie behind their development.

Before we became a nation of gardeners divisions in society meant that gardens were accessible only to the privileged. Pleasure was undoubtedly taken from the cultivation and observation of plants, such as cultivation by the florists, but leisure time was sparse for the majority until the reformations of the nineteenth century. In contrast to many other parts of the country landowners wealth was derived increasingly from industrial activity, particularly coal mining. In common with the fashion of the time they created landscaped parks befitting their position. As industrial growth escalated problems of overcrowded living conditions in towns were of national concern, none more so than the rapid growth within the Tyne and Wear river corridors. Reforms of burial procedures heralded the cemetery movement and shortly afterwards further concerns for the health of town dwellers were addressed by the building of public parks. Parks and gardens rapidly became established as part of everyday life. Housing, institutional and even industrial developments began to address their settings and provide an attractive environment for residents and workers. In addition to their visual contribution parks and gardens provided centres for entertainment, recreation, education, horticultural and technological advancement as well as a means of instilling moral values. The particular vagaries of the climate in the region provided a challenge for the designer. Denes and quarries were favoured but if no means of shelter existed protection was provided by the planting of tree belts and the construction of walled enclosures.

Inevitably many of the examples cited have been lost or adapted to the demands of the day. Whilst it is not appropriate or possible to stop the clock on a historic but living landscape, it is important to understand the significance of their distinctive qualities as they reflect the regions rich heritage which we should value.

The Historic Parks and Gardens of Tyne and Wear : The Gazetteer

Locations

Entries have been given a National Grid Reference where appropriate. Lost sites have a grey tone added to the background. It must be noted that some of the sites are private and there is no public access unless specified. Parks and Gardens included in the English Heritage Register of Historic Parks and Gardens are marked ❖

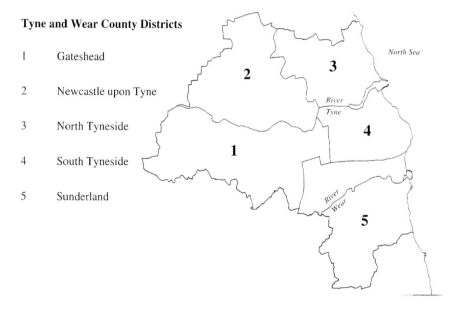

Tyne and Wear County Districts

1   Gateshead

2   Newcastle upon Tyne

3   North Tyneside

4   South Tyneside

5   Sunderland

Acknowledgements

Warmest thanks to; Ian Ayris, Harry Beamish, Eileen Carnaffin, Steve Desmond, Huw Dixon, Durham County Record Office, Simon Green, Barbara Harbottle, Colin Haylock, Ken Hutchinson, Dr. Harriet Jordan, Literary and Philosophical Society Newcastle upon Tyne, Local Studies Librarians at Gateshead Metropolitan Borough Council Library, Newcastle upon Tyne City Libraries, North of England Open Air Museum - Beamish, North Tyneside Central Library, South Tyneside Central Library, Sunderland Library, Northumberland County Record Office, David Lovie, Mike Lowe, Christine Matten, Les Milne, Martin Roberts, S.G.S. Environment Royston Thomas, Tyne & Wear Archive Services, University of Durham Archives and Special Collections, University of Newcastle upon Tyne, Robinson Library, Anthony Walker and Partners, Dr. Margaret Wills, Dr. T. Yellowley.

PICTURE CREDITS

Gateshead Metropolitan Borough Libraries and Arts, Newcastle City Libraries and Arts, Newcastle City Council, Northumberland County Record Office, SGS Environment, Tyne & Wear Archive Services, Anthony Walker and Partners.

The Historic Parks and Gardens of Tyne and Wear : Contents

EARLY PARKS, GARDENS AND HORTICULTURE

God Almightie first planted a Garden. And indeed, it is the Purest of Humane pleasures. It is the Greatest Refreshment to the Spirits of Man; Without which, Buildings and Pallaces are but Grosse Handy-works: And a man shall ever see, that when Ages grow to Civility and Elegancie, Men come to Build Stately, sooner then to Garden Finely: As if Gardening were the Greater Perfection. **Frances Bacon (1625).**

EARLY PARKS & GARDENS

The privilege of creating a deer park was restricted to those conferred with a royal licence. The licence was called the *Right of Saltory or Saltatorium* referring to permission to construct a deer-leap or saltory; a device which enabled deer to jump into the park but not out. Many affluent merchants were keen to improve their status and created deer parks which excluded local people from land which had previously been accessible to all. Maintaining a deer park was expensive; the oak pales surrounding the land were costly, building earth banks was labour intensive and the requirements of enclosed deer were not compatible with woodland husbandry. Keepers had to be employed such as Roger Tickhill in 1348 at **Bishop's Park**, Gateshead. The park extended across the east of Gateshead and was enclosed by a bank and ditch. Other deer parks south of the River Tyne were at **Hedworth, Barmston** (owned by the Hylton family), **Heworth, Lamesley** (owned in 1353 by Eleanor lady of Ravensheulme) and **Ravensworth** which was enclosed by licence granted to Sir Henry Fitzhugh by Richard II in 1391. Across the river at **Scotswood**, Richard Scot obtained a licence to enclose his 200 acre wood in Benwell. Records suggest the locals were not pleased by this and periodically helped themselves to wood, coal, cattle, deer, corn, hay and poached herons from their nests.

The landscapers later attempted to use or recreate deer parks as symbols of ancient lineage and left venerable old trees to give an air of authenticity.

Chopwell Woods were described by Ryan in his *History of Shotley Spa* as Crown lands, meaning land which was taken over by the Crown on the dissolution of the monasteries during the 1530s. Bourne suggested in his *History of Ryton* that the popular Ryton Ferry which ran from The Willows, originated from Cistercians at Morpeth who needed a crossing to administer their land at Chopwell. The valuable woodland was ministered for a time by the capable forester William Billington whose book *A Series of Facts Hints and Observations and Experiments on Raising Young Plantations from Acorn Seedlings and Larger Plants,* (1825), was no doubt extremely influential as it was subscribed to by many landowners such as Surtees who resided nearby at Hamsterley Hall. The woodland was deciduous at that time but is now mostly planted with conifers. The woods remain accessible through permission of the Forestry Authority.

Self sufficiency and security have not been easy over the centuries. Perhaps this is why the British waited until life was a little easier before they devoted their talents to gardening. Early references to gardening suggest that the aesthetic pleasure of gardens was restricted to those who were affluent enough to have leisure time. Whereas the general population were concerned with the functional use of plants as food or remedies.

In 1856 *Whellan's Directory* refers to many religious communities in Newcastle. West of Pilgrim Street a Franciscan convent had twelve acres of ground in the centre of town. According to Whellan gardens and tree plantations suffered *on account of the smoke which has for so many ages enveloped this town*. Ecclesiastical gardens would have been strictly utilitarian, growing fruit, vegetables and plants used for medicine or flavouring. One such plant, *Crocus sativus*, has been grown through the centuries for the scented stigma which when dried become saffron. Today we associate saffron cultivation with Spain, however it was widely cultivated throughout the country in the middle ages and used as a dye. Also for flavouring and medicinally. In 1939 the Gateshead historian, Mr. Oxberry noted a reference to a *Saffron Garden* at Bottle Bank in 1782.

Celia Fiennes visited Newcastle during the course of her journeys late in the seventeenth century. She described the **Barber Surgeons Hall** at Manors which *had a pretty garden walled in, full of flowers and greenes in potts and in the borders.* In 1736 Bourne wrote of the garden as having a square divided into four grassed sections, each containing a statue, to be contemplated from gravel walks.

An amusing reference to a garden in Newcastle comes from the historian Brand who visited the castle in 1778. He was surprised to find on the top of the castle keep *a little artificial garden producing apple trees, rose bushes and so on. Here a modest type of horticulture flourished for many years after this period and the tenant used facetiously to describe the interior of the castle, which was then roofless, as a large pit in the middle of his garden.*

Barber Surgeons Hall at Manors, Newcastle upon Tyne during the eighteenth century.

Section One ~~~~~~~~~~~~~~~~~ Early Parks, Gardens and Horticulture

While ordinary mortals concentrated on subsistence, the peerage were able to devote attention to laying out their grounds. Recent attention to the landscape at **Hylton Castle** in Sunderland has provoked much speculation. Although a chapel was recorded in 1157 and the village was referred to in 1323, the castle was not built until c.1395-1405 by Baron William Hylton. Through techniques of remote sensing, traces of earthworks have been revealed which suggest formal gardens dating from c.1650. Outline remains of buildings at Hylton have also been discovered and it is conjectured that they were associated with the gardens. The significance of these suggestions cannot be interpreted until archaeological investigations have progressed further.

Hylton Castle , Sunderland c. 1820.

The first edition O.S. map shows the castle set in open landscape punctuated by a scattering of individual trees to the south. The chapel overlooks the castle on a terrace and the second edition O.S. shows further terraced ground directly south. A canal has been uncovered in Hylton Dene and both first and second edition O.S. maps show perfunctory looking walks along the dene. A wall runs east-west but whether it was built to retain the banks or be ornamental is not known.

In contrast to the early manor gardens those built during the 1600s penetrated the wider landscape. Designs continued to be restrained but were more elaborate with linear paths, knots, topiary and clipped hedges. The Italian Renaissance gardens began to influence European gardens although this was a trend which would have taken some time to reach gardens of lesser nobility. Usually the house took precedence on a mound with small enclosed gardens to each side of the building. A terrace was constructed to overlook a wide lawn with further terraces and avenued walks. Water gardens were important, technical difficulties however, often caused stagnation, an irritation to the garden philosopher Francis Bacon who mentioned the problem in his essay **Of Gardens** (1625).

Looking at the early maps and plans of towns such as Newcastle, gardens and orchards feature prominently. Corbridge's map of Newcastle (1723), shows Sir William Blackett's house, Anderson Place with extensive gardens. An engraving by Kip c.1715 gives a bird's eye view of the gardens adjacent to the town walls. Although the grounds were not vast a feeling of space and the opportunity for many vistas were given by formal arrangements of orchards, parterres, terraces, statues and numerous tree lined walks. A building which could have been a banqueting house or gazebo is shown on the north boundary. When Major Anderson died in 1831 Richard Grainger bought Anderson Place and The Nuns, an adjacent property, in order to begin his scheme to provide direct routes across the city with the new streets Grey Street, Grainger Street and Clayton Street.

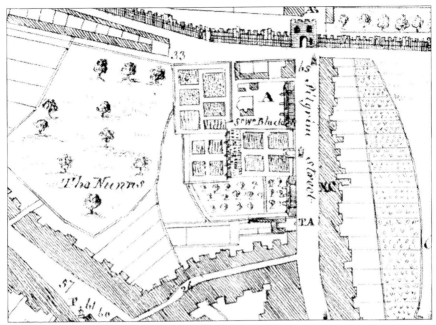

Anderson Place, Newcastle upon Tyne, Corbridge's Map 1723.

Inset of Blacketts House, Corbridge's Map 1723.

As a result of the rapid expansion of the towns in Tyne & Wear there are many landscapes which have been lost. Park Estate and Redheugh Estate were both depicted on 1857 O.S. maps of Gateshead, showing extensive landscaped grounds. **Park Estate** or **Gateshead Park** was originally part of the Bishop of Durham's deer park. However, by the time William Cotesworth became lord of the manor in 1716 the acreage had diminished. Cotesworth spent vast sums on improvements to the estate and later his son in law, Henry Ellison, also made improvements. His garden accounts of 1733 read *Making a plantation on the west side of the new kitchen garden £5. 2s. 9 ¼ d.* John Harvey in his definitive account *Early Nurserymen* recorded that Stephen Switzer the renowned writer and garden designer was very keen to work on Gateshead Park and even attempted to oust the resident gardener.

The house was approached from the north as the road entered an oval shaped turning drive lined with trees and shrubs. To the south front a terrace gave views over small diamond and circular shapes which may have been a parterre. Thick plantations of trees enclosed the park. West of the house a canal ran parallel with the walled garden. As is common with many northern walled gardens the structure is rhomboidal being wider at the southern end to maximise the effect of sunlight on the east and west walls.

GATESHEAD PARK HOUSE
The Seat of Isac Cockson Esq.

Gateshead Park House, c.1820.

Redheugh was an ancient estate which belonged to the Redheugh family since before the thirteenth century. By 1713 the land had passed out of the family and subsequent occupants managed to resist William Cotesworth's desires to purchase the land to extend his coal rights. Richardson's *Descriptive Companion to Newcastle upon Tyne* (1838), stated *The garden, pleasure grounds and plantations are laid out with great taste*. The land was purchased from Cuthbert Ellison in 1836 and by the time it was illustrated on the 1st edition O.S. map a designed layout was established. On the western aspect of the grounds plantations shielded the railway which ran parallel to the River Tyne. The southern end of the gardens were on a steep bank which ran along the boundary. The kitchen gardens were protected by sections of wall rather than an entire enclosure. To the south front of the house the lawn was divided by irregular shaped beds. Serpentine walks led around the kitchen gardens, from lawns into woodland, and overlooking parkland to the east. Eventually the railway and industrial activity along the river interfered with enjoyment of the house and it was no longer suitable as a gentleman's residence. In 1850 the estate was offered for sale with a view to capitalising on the shortage of building land but this was unsuccessful and the house sank into decay and was finally demolished in the 1930s.

Drawn by J Sopwith

REDHEUGH HOUSE,
The Residence of W.ᵐ Cuthbert Esq.ʳ

Published May 1829 by W.Davison Alnwick .

Redheugh House, Gateshead c.1820.

COMMON LAND - RECREATION

An aerial view of **Medieval England** would have shown a country divided into small rural communities with few towns. As communications improved a stop over point was required in each village to rest livestock and provide a meeting or trading place. Many of the village greens which developed have survived and reflect the early settlement patterns of villages around them.

Southwick Green forms a centre for the original settlement of Southwick. Despite popularity as a residential area for industrialists the green was a dustbowl by 1909 and it was proposed to tar it over. By 1912 the council took control of the green from the ecclesiastical commissioners and in 1913 Robert Thompson a Southwick shipbuilder, paid for a park to be laid out in memory of his father. The 'fore-end' of the park was laid out in the form of a ship. In 1984 a Police Station was built on part of the green.

Whitburn has a village green with a raised area, The Bank, forming the east part on Front Street. Nearby is a Pin-fold, a pound for stray cattle.

Ryton village green provides an attractive heart to the village. A cross dated 1795, marked a meeting place at Ryton for farm labourers at the beginning of the hiring seasons in May and November. Riotous fairs were held on the green but were abandoned after 1866.

Charleton described **Shieldfield Green** as an area where troops congregated prior to a battle with the Scots in 1547. The fort which stood there was a key position during the siege of 1644. Charleton also tells the story of King Charles playing golf on the green during his captivity in Newcastle. Despite the historic nature of the site by 1750 most of the land had been adopted by adjacent landowners.

Commons, or the land on extremities of cultivated areas, were of little consequence to manors until they escalated in value once the pressure for land grew due to expansion of towns. There were lengthy battles between the local people and those who sought to enclose the land, not only because of the principle of losing their commons but because civic space, frequently used for recreation, was also being eradicated. The very people who had profited from the new building and industrial expansion returned land to the local people in a different package, as benefactors, seeking to improve the health and also the attitudes of their workers by giving them parks.

The origins of the rights of Newcastle Freemen to use the **Town Moor** are unclear and this may be why rights to access were frequently in dispute. In 1772 the Freemen were incensed when part of the Moor was offered by the Corporation for lease. A bill was eventually passed by Parliament allowing Freemen or their widows to graze two milking cows on the moor. Other parts were retained for communal use for fairs, horse racing, military drilling and cultivation.

Thomas Sopwith in *The Strangers Pocket Guide to Newcastle upon Tyne* (1838) wrote, *The town moor is easily accessible and open common, over which the stranger may freely range.*

The Cheviot Hills are very conspicuous in clear weather, as are the moors of Rimside, and the serrated edge of Simonside to the north. On the east the geologist will trace the bold escarpment of the magnesian limestone, overlying the long extended plains of the coal district near Boldon. On the south is Gateshead fell surmounted by a tall spire. West of it is the fertile valley of the Team, with the adjoining hills, and woods and castle of Ravensworth.

Sunderland Moor provides an example of the natural inclination of a community to adopt a space as a point for congregating. The traditional activities held on the moor reflect the preoccupations of the city; horse racing, bull baiting, quoits and bowling, drying and bleaching linen, drying fishing nets and as a meeting place for sailors and keelmen. A pond near the edge of the moor was used for watering horses and ice skating in winter. The moor was used as a point for defence and housed early eighteenth century forts and gun emplacements.

Building Hill in Sunderland has long been an important site in the city. One reason for this was the view which was afforded of the harbour. The hill also provided a suitable point for beacons to be lit. When Paul Jones, a notorious pirate, sailed into the mouth of the River Wear fires were said to be lit on the hill as a warning. The hill had been quarried by copyholders, who were sanctioned to quarry stone for building and James Burnett in 1830 wrote that much of Bishopwearmouth had been built in this manner. A rather exaggerated view from here was painted by John Storey in 1856 showing Mowbray Park shortly after it was built.

Windmill Hills in Gateshead was a traditional meeting place and during the early eighteenth century was a popular racecourse. Hoppings were held on the hill at Whitsun with activities such as wrestling, and ludicrous games such as running after a cheese with the pursuant tied in a sack! Windmill Hills gradually became more and more popular as a park. However, it was not suggested as a site for a Peoples Park until 1857 and became Gateshead's first public park in 1859.

Numerous denes in the county have been used for recreation. In North Tyneside, **Holywell Dene** continues to be used by locals. Many public parks were built in denes taking advantage of the shelter provided from prevailing winds as well as the aesthetic advantages of the landscape. They were filled in to provide further land for building. **Pandon Dene** in Newcastle survived with a network of bridges forming connections for important parts of the city. Charleton was dismayed by the intrusion of modern requirements for the land which was gradually lost to railway development and tipping of rubbish. *There was the lovely valley, with the burn winding through it- the hum of water mills and the song of the birds amongst the trees coming pleasantly upwards to the ear. The mass of apple blossom and the teeming luxuriance of the foliage which covered the banks, the little summer-houses in the trim gardens, and the winding pathway from the town to the Shieldfied, formed a picture of rare sylvan beauty.*

Marden Quarry, in North Tyneside was opened as a nature reserve in 1977. William Weaver Tomlinson wrote in 1893 *Sixty or seventy years ago, before the limestone was worked out so much, there were pretty islets surrounded by willows in the quarry pond, and fiddlers used to sit on them on fine summer evenings playing merry tunes, while young people came from the* *surrounding district to dance on the soft green turf. The pond at the time was full of tench and afforded sport to the village anglers.*

Horse racing has always been a popular sport in the region and the race course on Killingworth Moor was a favourite location from the early 1600s. In 1721 the venue was changed to Newcastle Town Moor and the Town of Newcastle donated a gold cup as a prize. On June 25th 1838 the first race for the Northumberland Plate was held. The course was moved to Gosforth Park in 1881. The races were very popular and drew vast numbers of spectators from all walks of life.

In Sunderland, horse racing was also held on the Town Moor and one of the last occasions was in 1732 when prizes amounting to £110 were awarded. Later horse racing was held at Tunstall Hope and a painting depicting this scene can be viewed at Sunderland Museum.

A famous racecourse was at Blaydon, the first races being held on Newburn Haughs in 1811. After a series of locations the races were moved to Blaydon Island (now gone) where public transport was provided by the railway, steamers, buses and a floating bridge made of keel boats. The excitement of the day was fuelled by steady consumption of liquor which continued well into the night and ....*Some had black eyes and broken shins, An some lay drunk among the whins, A Comin frae the Races!* (Blaydon Races).

Bowling was a favourite pastime often played at inns by people from all realms of society. Bowls themselves were usually made of blue stone picked up on the beach then chipped with hammer and worked smooth on other stone. The Sunderland keelmen had a reputation of being the most skilful players. Celia Fiennes (1685 - 1712) visited Newcastle in 1694 and wrote *There is a very pleasant bowling-green a little walk out of the town with a large gravel walke round it with two rows of trees on each side making it very shady; there is a fine entertaineing house that makes up the fourth side before which is a paved walke under pyasoes (piazzas) of bricke; there is a pretty garden by the side shady walk, its a sort of Spring Garden where the Gentlemen and Ladyes walke in the evening; there is a green house in the garden.*

The 1898 O.S. map for Ryton indicates a **Curling Pond** in the grounds of Ryton Grove opposite the railway station. Another was shown in Hebburn, (NZ 308647), now built over by industrial works. Curling involves sliding heavy circular shaped stones across ice; although still popular in Scotland the game has lost favour in England.

HORTICULTURE

One of the most important traditions was the culture of plants by **florists**. Once the deluge of new plants had been introduced to gardens it became fashionable to develop plant collections. In turn, the temptation to *improve* plant material was taken up with great enthusiasm. Once a value for the new plants was established the passion turned to mania and transactions incurring vast sums were common. Plants exhibited by the florists included carnation, tulip, anemone, ranunculus, auricula, hyacinth, polyanthus, pink, and after 1830 the pansy and dahlia were added. The plants were exhibited at Florists Feasts such as one advertised in the Newcastle Chronicle in 1777, *This is to give Notice to all Florifts and lovers of gardening, That the Gardener and Gentlemen Florifts intend to hold their meeting for the show of carnations, and adjuding Prizes to the moft excellent, at Mr Edw. Cowling's at the Foot of the Groat-market, on Monday the firft Day of September, at Two o' Clock; where the expense of cold entertainment will be made as moderate as poffible. And it is hoped, many Lovers of this innocent Amufement will favour them with their company, and join themfelves Members of this Society.* It was easy for anyone to cultivate florists plants as little space was required for a few pots. Walter White visited a gardener in St. Anthony's in Walker in 1859. *Guided by the towering chimney, I sought Locke and Blackett's lead-works. It was an agreeable surprise to find a garden inside the great gates, and an old gardener fondling his beds of pinks. The flowers came pretty well he said, though t'was smokey; and twas a pleasure to look after'em when he was not wanted in the works.* The florists of the region were famous for their expertise. A particular favourite was a gold laced polyanthus *Bark's Bonny Bess* also called the Queen of the Days that are Gone. Newspapers frequently advertised sales of bulbs imported from Holland. In 1834 an auctioneer offered *One box of prime Dutch Flower roots, containing double and single Hyacinths, double and single Jonquils, Iris, Crocus, double and single Narcissus and Anemones; also a choice and valuable assortment of white and yellow ground Tulips all named; and a very choice assortment of Ranunculas, of many different colours, one of each named. The above are well worth the attention of all florists.*

The Botanical and Horticultural Society for Durham, Northumberland and Newcastle upon Tyne was founded in 1824. Smaller societies also existed and in Seaton Sluice a Flower Show was held in September 1840. Having recorded the proceedings of the exhibition the correspondent launched into an appreciation of the society. *Although we are reckoned a kind of 'stand still' community at Seaton Sluice, we can boast of this one society, which affords proof of improvement, as we are certain cockfighting, bowling, & co, are fast giving way to more rational amusements. A library - something in the shape of a mechanics institution - would do much for this neighbourhood, and we hope shortly to have it in our power to number ourselves among those who are on the "March of Intellect".*

A very successful exhibitor at the Botanical and Horticultural Society for Durham, Northumberland and Newcastle upon Tyne was Adam Hogg who worked for Messrs. Falla & Co. Nurserymen, Gateshead. William Falla I had worked at William Joyces nursery but moved to Thompson's at Pickhill in Bedale on Joyce's death in 1771. During Falla's absence the nursery was taken over by George Dale but on his demise Falla returned and bought the lease, all the stock and the valuable goodwill already resting on the business.

Joyce and Dale were both prominent nurserymen dealing with large orders from the wealthy estates funded by the coal trade. Joyce settled on Tyneside after laying out Wallington in Northumberland, his business developed through supplying plants, laying out landscapes and advising on these matters. His catalogue was used by Joseph Spence when laying out the grounds at Finchale Priory c.1755. This document survives and is now known to be one of the earliest catalogues with prices.

Falla continued the tradition of catalogues and these have provided a wealth of information on plant material of the period. When William Falla II suceeded to the business in 1804 he disposed of the nursery at Hebburn Quay and bought 130 acres of land at Carr Hill. He managed to expand his business by producing such large quantities of stock that he was able to undercut other enterprises. Landowners were planting woodland for profit, enclosure of land required hedging of boundaries, and c.1814 he won a contract to replant 900 acres of Chopwell forest. Falla's nursery became the largest in the country as he continued to supply trees to replace woodland which sustained the ever growing demands of industry including shipbuilding and mining. William Falla II died in 1830 and his son William Falla III succeeded to the nursery which extended by this time to over 500 acres. The business floundered and William Falla III disappeared in April 1836. The *Local Historians Table Book* recorded subsequent events, *The body of Mr. Wm. Falla, nurseryman in Gateshead, who had been missing since the 2nd of April, and of whom nothing had been heard from that period, notwithstanding a very diligent search was accidentally discovered lying in Ravensworth Wood, near Lamesley, where according to the verdict of a respectable jury he had 'destroyed himself in a fit of temporary insanity'.*

One of the most famous traditions of the county is allotment gardening. **Allotments** in cities were worked by people from all classes whereas in the country they fed the poorest families. In Gateshead the allotments at Shipcote were started in 1894 with encouragement from the Rural Labourer's League, a land reform organisation. The allotments on Newcastle Town Moor have continued the tradition of the right for local people to cultivate common land. In many old pit villages former colliery houses still retain the distinctive allotment strip behind each house. Many had a pig sty at the furthest end. Pit families balanced food production with leisure. Vegetables, especially leeks, were cultivated along with flowers such as dahlias and chrysanthemums; all types of produce were exhibited at Horticultural Shows. Pigeons have continued to enthuse allotment holders and wheeling flights of the birds are a common sight as are the painted *lofts* or *crees* built in an optimum position to guide the birds back from racing.

LANDSCAPED PARKS

Spurred on by increasing wealth and relative political security, landowners in the eighteenth century were quick to adopt the vogue for designing an estate that would reflect their status. Many 'landscaped parks' remain today, often making a great impact as mature trees stand out in todays open farmland. Elderly belts of woodland can still provide evidence of estate boundaries even though all traces of buildings have been removed.

Landowners were able to increase their estates through enclosure and because tax on land was reduced. They arranged for the disposal of any intrusion on their privacy and were not above removing evidence of settlements, relocating inhabitants elsewhere, sometimes devising a model village. Roads and footpaths were also diverted to stop 'unsavoury characters' passing close by the house.

Following the influences of seventeenth century Europe manifested by intricate parterres, water, topiary, statues and so on, a new consciousness began to develop in this country. The loosening of ties with European trends triggered a reaction against the tight geometric organisation of landscape and the 'Englishness' of our landscape began to develop. The early eighteenth century was a time of discovery for those participating in the Grand Tour. The impact of these experiences inspired a new consciousness which was reinforced by artists such as Salvator Rosa and Claude who depicted classical Italian landscape with human figures diminished by scenery. Pope and Addison, two major writers of the period, propounded a new attitude towards gardening, rejecting the monotonous regularity of formal gardens and encouraging the idea that qualities which existed naturally should determine the form of a garden. Pope's dictum from his *Epistle to Burlington* (1731) was *In all, let nature never be forgot....Consult the Genius of the Place.*

Designers such as Kent gave the wilderness classical elements; buildings, bridges, ruins, devices which provided a framework to direct the eye across the view. Man held the reins for nature in a most contrived and contradictory way.

Paradoxically, Walpole's obituary for Capability Brown read, *such, however, was the effect of his genius that when he was the happiest man, he will be least remembered; so closely did he copy nature that his works will be mistaken.* The scene was in fact as ordered as a painting, having been conquered, idealised and well managed.

As well as views from the generous windows of the Georgian house the sensation of a park was designed to be perceived on the move, on horseback or in carriages from the rides around the park. The landscape was designed to indicate the patrons impeccable taste and intellect. Landowners were often portrayed standing in a family group with the park behind, by painters such as Gainsborough.

Dunston Hill, Gateshead.

North eastern gardens do not feature prominently in guides to gardens in Britain. However, distinguished garden designers have originated from the region. Thomas Wright (1711 - 86), was born at Byers Green, Co. Durham. Although a contemporary of Brown he offered a completely different vision, his designs being elaborate and in Rococo style. 'Capability' Brown (1716 - 83), remarkably, remains a household name almost 200 years after his death. He was born at Kirkharle in Northumberland where he developed his expertise working for Sir William Loraine. Robert Shafto heard of Brown's talent and commissioned him to layout the grounds of Benwell Tower c.1738. Formerly a country seat of the Priors of Tynemouth, only a few trees remain and the area is densely built up. Brown's career developed quickly and he moved south to numerous major commissions such as Blenheim, Petworth, and Longleat. He returned to work on the parkland at Alnwick in 1760 and the lakes at Rothley near Wallington in 1765. Brown's influence has been strong in the region and it has been conjected that he worked directly on schemes for Wallington and Hesleyside. Certainly Brown had many followers such as Thomas White who worked on Lumley Castle in 1768 and moved to Butsfield in Co. Durham in 1800.

As Brown's career escalated, his design principles and themes became well established. His approach was applied consistently to each commission. The estate would be bounded by perimeter planting and often a small stream was damned unobtrusively to form a lake. The view to and from the house was cleared of visual intrusions such as flower gardens, kitchen gardens, and the lawns appeared to flow from the house itself, having been cleverly separated by a sunken fence or *ha-ha*. The landscape was opened out and walls around the house were removed. This required some degree of bravery in the region as border raids were not comfortably in the past.

Although Repton (1752-1818) is credited with continuing Brown's tradition he frequently improved much smaller landscapes. He became adept at techniques of illusion and making estates appear larger. Instead of using a *ha-ha* to separate the garden from pasture he often accentuated the transition by building terraces and including flower beds on lawns. Repton is not recorded as having worked in Durham, Northumberland or Cumbria, nevertheless, he was very influential as he published literature on his schemes, such as *Sketches and Hints* c.1795.

Early landscaped parks in Tyne and Wear often involved land reclamation after mining activity. Ravensworth Castle and Dunston Hill have remains of bell pits which have been found disguised by tree plantations. These plantations would also have provided screening of the increasing industrial activity in the Tyne Valley.

GIBSIDE ❖ — GATESHEAD : NZ 180590

It is the pleasure of people of taste in the north to pay an annual visit to Gibside Woods remarked the Newcastle Chronicle in 1756 and so, over 200 years later, it remains today. Gibside is a majestic eighteenth century landscape and the very special qualities the estate possesses have become far more accessible to the public in recent years with the purchase of the remaining Strathmore interest by the National Trust. Recent research has revealed both previously unappreciated complexities in the landscape and the scale of the engineering works involved..

Gibside Hall was built between 1603 and 1620 by William Blakiston and is thought to replace a yet earlier building. It was built on a steep slope above the Derwent Valley, a similar escarpment position to the medieval fortified manor of Old Hollinside to the north. The Gibside we know today did not really begin to develop until the estate was inherited by George Bowes in 1722. Over the next forty five years he created a landscape on an epic scale, using some of the great wealth he was accumulating as one of the major coal owners in the area. The core of the landscape design consists of a series of intersecting axial avenues allowing lengthy and striking views. Buildings and other features were used to terminate these views and at places where the avenues intersect. Perhaps the key fulcrum of this layout is a mound, which acts as a *rond point*, where axes intersect, though forestry planting and the cutting of a forestry road now makes it's significance hard to appreciate. However, it is placed at the north end of *The Hollow Walk* on the principal and most spectacular axis which connects the Chapel and Monument and includes the Grand Walk. To the north should be a vista over the Round Pond down towards Lady Haugh and to the south east up over the Octagon Pond to the Banqueting House on the brow of the hill. Cutting through the formal layout is a serpentine drive (1738 - 40), designed to allow brief and changing views of the various features of the Estate as the Hall is approached.

There has long been speculation on who designed Gibside. There is a reference in Estate papers to payments to Stephen Switzer for preparing at least one plan. Switzer was a very notable landscape designer and writer of the early eighteenth century. Whether or not he

Engraving of Gibside (after Turner)

planned the landscape, or whether George Bowes in fact planned his own layout, the design certainly seems to follow Switzer's principles. His style represents a compromise between continental formality and the informal English parkland then being developed. Switzer believed in incorporating a whole estate within a design and that this was to be best accomplished by establishing one or two great axial lines, or *boldest strokes*. Another important figure in evolving the design was William Joyce who after being dismissed as gardener acted as a kind of visiting clerk of works, advising on technical matters.

Bowes adorned his landscape with a series of magnificent buildings. Two principal architects were employed, both of national standing: Daniel Garrett until his death in 1753, when he was replaced by James Paine. The first building of consequence developed by Bowes was the *Bath House* (possibly by Garrett), constructed between 1733 and 1736. Only foundations of this survive today though the site is marked and stands at the top of an impressive retaining wall above the River Derwent. Next came the *Banqueting House* in 1741 - 44 and Stables 1747 - 51, both documented as by Garrett. The former is a pretty whimsical *gothick* building. It sits overlooking the valley above a series of terraces leading down to the Octagon Pond. The Column of Liberty was started in 1750 by Garrett and finished in 1757 by Paine. Representing liberty, the Column was an expression of Bowes Whig politics. The female figure is dressed in classical drapery and carries the staff of maintenance and the cap of liberty. The column is over 140 feet high and at the time it was exceeded in height only by Sir Christopher Wren's Monument in London. Gibside Chapel is the finest building of all on the estate. It was started in 1760, the year of George Bowes' death. It is Paine's ecclesiastical masterpiece and perhaps the finest Palladian church in the country.

Many other notable features survive from George Bowes' era, for example the walled garden adjacent to the grand walk, which was laid out ornamentally. There is also a well preserved *ice house*. After Bowes' death further developments were mainly complementary to the character which he had established. This is one of the factors that makes Gibside such a special place; the temptation to remodel the Estate to modern tastes was avoided leaving Gibside a very well preserved landscape of the early to mid eighteenth century. The main building project after Bowes' death was the construction of an orangery in 1772 - 74, south along the escarpment from the Hall, and viewed from the Grand Walk. This was built for Mary Eleanor Bowes, George Bowes' only child who married the ninth Earl of Strathmore. Through the years various modifications were undertaken to the Hall, most substantially a major remodelling in 1805 by Alexander Gilkie.

Planting was used at Gibside to give a series of visual contrasts between, for example, dense woodland and open parkland and broad vistas and confined serpentine walks. Eighteenth and nineteenth century planting only survives in pockets and is dominated by modern forestry planting. In addition to woodland blocks, trees were used ornamentally; it seems that the serpentine drive may have been lined with yew and that limes were used to line one of the vistas. There are also the remnants of nineteenth century specimen tree planting around the Estate using species such as Wellingtonia, for example, around the Octagon Pond.

Following a visit to Gibside in 1753, the Dean of Durham wrote to his brother *Last week I was at Glory Bowes's at Gibside, to do it justice, I think it will be one of the finest places in the North when he has finish'd his design. The whole of his works takes in a range of seven miles; which if ever completed will be worthy of his Magnificence and Immensity.*

After a long decline Gibside is now being revived by the National Trust. Though it is never likely to be restored completely to the condition of it's heyday, the work the Trust is undertaking is gradually revealing a great landscape design.

A book on Gibside, *Gibside and the Bowes Family* by Dr. Margaret Wills is forthcoming.

ACCESS PROVIDED BY NATIONAL TRUST. Spectacular views can be seen from the Derwent Walk.

AXWELL PARK ❖ — GATESHEAD : NZ 191620

Axwell Park, along with Gibside, is one of the two great estates of the Derwent Valley. Axwell Park was developed by Sir Thomas Clavering and seems to have been a conspicuous attempt to compete for status and prestige with George Bowes at Gibside. The house at Axwell Park is central to the landscape design, whereas at Gibside it is one element in a complex whole. It also represents developing landscape tastes, with a far more informal approach compared to the strong axial vistas employed at Gibside.

The house was designed in 1758 by the nationally renowned Palladian architect James Paine who had already worked at Gibside and was, shortly afterwards, to design Gibside Chapel. Clavering repeatedly interfered and altered Paine's designs, to such an extent that in his published memoirs Paine wrote a long complaint against Clavering and lamented having become involved in the project. His altered designs were executed by John Bell of Durham. Once Clavering was elected an M.P. for Durham in 1768 he spent much of his time in London and the development of Axwell is likely to have slowed or stopped. The house and garden subsequently experienced two phases of activity before the eventual sale of the estate in 1920. About 1815 - 20 John Dobson was employed by the next Clavering's French wife, Claire Gallais. His contribution included building a garden temple, since destroyed. Later in the 1880s Henry Augustus Clavering, the 10th and last Baronet, undertook a meticulous restoration of the estate.

Very little is known about the laying out of the landscape. In essence it is typical of the mid to late eighteenth century, enclosed within a walled estate and laid out as parkland, combined with blocks of woodland. The Hall has two principal elevations, the north east and the south east, both of which faced open parkland. The view to the north east, effectively *the garden front*, would have been virtually unimpeded down to the lake (which survives), a contrived feature in the middle distance. Beyond are more distant views of the Tyne Valley. Overlooking the lake is a fine open *gothick* Dower House. The views to the south east, from the *entrance front*, would have been of woodland along the north western bank of the serpentine lake and towards Whickham beyond. Nineteenth century additions to the landscape, presumably by Henry Clavering, include a *pleasure ground* of walks through exotic trees and shrubs and a formal terrace around the Hall. The estate has sadly declined since it's sale in 1920 and significant intrusions have taken place including housing both on the approach to the Hall and between it and the lake.

NO PUBLIC ACCESS

RAVENSWORTH CASTLE — GATESHEAD : NZ 230590

This massive park, comprising of over 800 acres, was enclosed by licence to Sir Henry Fitzhugh by Richard II c.1391. A castle has been on the site since the twelfth century. The park was mentioned in a deed of 1356 when John Lumley granted Robert Umfravill *the site, demesne, park, meadows and pasture of the manor of Rauenshelme* for a term, and with the right to work coal.

The first house was built within the castle in 1724, and improved by Paine c.1759. An early eighteenth century garden plan shows an avenue with two further avenues branching to the side. Sir Henry Liddell sent his son patterns for seats and railings for the garden in 1723. He wrote later that year asking his son to think about plantations, where and how a canal or pond could be introduced and what suitable ornaments they would need. Whether any of these schemes were realised remains unclear.

In 1808 the house was demolished and John Nash, one of the foremost architects in the country, built a romantic, medieval castle style house. Despite being a most picturesque building in the medieval revival style it was demolished during the 1950s. The house stood on a substantial terrace enjoying views over parkland framed by planting. Ornamental gardens to the north west of the house are still discernable. Fine Cedar trees grow in the vicinity of the house but there is little sign of the arboretum shown on the 1898 O.S. map. An article published in *Gardener's Magazine* in 1834 describes the fine woodland and attraction of the

Ravensworth Castle, Gateshead late nineteenth century.

estate when viewed from Newcastle or Gateshead. An impression is given of the establishment by a description of the conservatory. This was entered through a secret door in the library when the surprised visitor suddenly found themselves *in the midst of odiferous plants, where they may contemplate the works of nature developing themselves in numerous forms.* Outside a terrace with a wide gravel wall overlooked lawns, flower beds and the old ivy clad castle. The castle walls gave protection to half hardy shrubs and climbers. The walled garden was approached by a variety of serpentine routes past *the finer kinds of shrubs.* The paths passed the fish pond which by that time had been adapted to house flamboyant wildfowl. The gardener was keen to follow the fashion for producing unusual vegetables and fruit from an array of glasshouses. Pine-stoves were used to grow pineapples, a fruit which requires temperatures above 80 degrees Fahrenheit, but this did not pose a problem on an estate which also ran collieries. The peach-houses were also kept warm by pipes heated by stoves. One greenhouse was devoted entirely to pelargoniums and a particularly successful variety was called *Lord Ravensworth.* Richardson's *Descriptive Companion to Newcastle upon Tyne,* 1838, described Ravensworth as *The gardens in which a most elegant range of hot houses, perhaps not inferior to any in the kingdom, display considerable taste.*

Existing planting basically follows the 1857 O.S. map. Conifers predominate in the belts and some parkland trees survive. A lodge and gateway (South Lodge) remain at the former principal entrance to the east and the drive is traceable. The park has an attractive home farm and other vernacular buildings of interest. Although the site is edged by the A1, housing and The Team Valley Trading Estate, the park is surprisingly intact.

NO PUBLIC ACCESS

BRADLEY PARK ❖ — GATESHEAD : NZ 125630

Walking across the fields to the south west of Bradley Park one could imagine oneself in the eighteenth century. In the foreground is attractive eighteenth century parkland; beyond the well preserved Bradley Hall.

The house was built c.1760 for John Simpson, a Newcastle merchant. The architect is unknown - it was long thought to have been James Paine but this was subsequently disproved. Dobson altered the house in 1813 for the first Lord Ravensworth. The hall is accompanied by many features typical of an eighteenth century estate. To the west are an orangery and an ice-house. To the south the hall is separated from the park by a *ha-ha.* A terrace runs alongside the wall which encloses a formal garden; for which a planting plan was drawn by J. Cook in 1842, providing rose beds and herbaceous borders. There is a small terrace to the south with a lawn. The stables and outbuildings to the north of the hall are enclosed by high walls. Other estate buildings include a large walled kitchen garden to the north east of the hall (now a commercial nursery open to visitors), and the Victorian North and South Lodges. The main area of parkland lies to the south and west of the hall. In the park vestigial remains of fishponds can be seen.

NO PUBLIC ACCESS. - PUBLIC FOOTPATH ADJACENT.

GOSFORTH PARK — NEWCASTLE UPON TYNE : NZ 250710

North Gosforth was acquired by the Brandling family in 1566. In 1760 Charles Brandling moved there from Felling and commissioned James Paine to design a house which would reflect the prominence of the Brandling family. As Brown was working in the 1760s at Alnwick and Rothley, one might conjecture that he collaborated to some extent with Paine who was disposed towards Brown's work at that time. Paine's book *Plans of Noblemen's and Gentlemen's Houses* published in 1767 was sympathetic to Brown's theories.

The park, by any standards, is vast, covering over 1000 acres, with the house located at the northern end. The 1858 O.S. map shows a number of interesting features. On the northern perimeter approaching Sandy Lane, an irregular shaped fish pond is situated in a position which does not suggest an ornamental feature. The kitchen garden is south of the pond, with an ice house, well insulated in woodland nearby. The house was given a prospect over open fields interspersed by clumps of trees with the lake in the far distance, on the south east side. The park was contained by dense woodland planting around its perimeter. A ha-ha separates the house from the parkland thereby allowing uninterrupted views. Circuits for rides begin from the house and radiate out around the park. In 1776 Hutchinson was overcome by admiration for the scheme, *no place in the county of Northumberland better ascertains the improvements in which the northern lands are capable. The great advancement which has taken place here is almost incredible, and the noble works which now fill a tract of land that was covered with heath and had all the dreary aspect of barrenness and waste are astonishing. To Mr. Brandling every lover of his country must return thanks for the example he has given to spur on emulation for improvement.*

George Stephenson lived in a cottage nearby at West Moor and was a family friend. Stephenson designed a lamp which through burning underwater attracted fish at night and he amused the family by fishing with the lamp in Gosforth Lake.

The Brandlings were a prominent Tory family and had many connections with other politicians in the area through marriage between local families. Sarah Brandling married Mathew Bell whose family seat at Woolsington Hall was nearby. The business interests of the family extended to collieries and a railway (which ran between Newcastle, South Shields and Sunderland). The estates became highly profitable through agricultural and mining returns. However, in 1852 the family were struck by financial disaster and the estate was broken up and sold in lots. The largest acreage including the house, went to Thomas Smith, a Tyneside shipbuilder. In 1880 the race course was established and the house was converted to a club and grandstand.

Although recent years have seen the decline of horse racing, the course remains one of the most important in the country. More recently an exhibition centre, golf course, nursery, and campsite have been developed.

LIMITED PUBLIC ACCESS.

SILKSWORTH HOUSE — now DOXFORD HOUSE
SUNDERLAND : NZ 375528

Doxford House garden was designed but is now a public park. Remaining estate walls and mature trees make a promising approach. On entering the park one loses the relationship between house and garden as the house is separated by a wall. A grassed embankment runs behind the house, sloping down to an awkwardly shaped, long and narrow pond. The water level appears to have dropped and this does little to enhance the problem of the modern day park. Lawns and tarmac compete with remnants of stone embellishments to the bank of the pond. The pond is a central feature to the layout of paths which lead to an area where a dene is formed by the stream feeding the pond. A walk through fields to the north leads to a kitchen garden with superb brick walls, some were used as *hot walls* for growing fruit, many flues are visible due to the deterioration of the structure. Today the walk runs through beech woods and a pleasant herbaceous and shrub border stands against the south wall of the kitchen garden. The house is on a higher level than most of the garden providing views across to trees in the parkland beyond. On the west side of the pond, an ice house has been recently discovered in a mound where the land rose up to the level of the fields. This was not annotated on the 1858 or 1896 O.S. maps, being possibly shrouded by undergrowth.

PUBLIC PARK.

WOOLSINGTON HALL ❖ — NEWCASTLE UPON TYNE
NZ 200705

Woolsington was mentioned as in the possession of Tynemouth Priory in Richard I's Charter in 1189 and the medieval village of Wulsingtona was probably near the site of the existing hall. Today, although Newcastle International Airport is a stone's throw away the park remains largely a product of the eighteenth century.

The first known depiction of the hall is on a map by Robertson in 1727. This shows a formal geometric garden to the south and east of the house, with a central path from the house directed past quartered rectangular beds to a pair of gates opening to the main drive. The east side of the formal garden was divided into a cross. A later map of 1744 shows a parterre laid out on the east side of the house with the previous layout removed.

In 1748 Mathew Bell bought the estate and his improvements are largely what remains today. The 1857 O.S. map shows a remarkably similar layout to the existing conditions with the exception that the south west corner has been developed for housing. The perimeter of the park is outlined by a ride along the shelter belts overlooking the parkland. A drive cuts north through the centre of the park from the south lodge with large clumps of trees dispersed either side. A fish pond bisects the park which reputedly provided carp and fresh mussels for the hall. This previously flowed over a cascade prior to a subsidence problem. The watercourse was crossed by an elegant stone bridge which continued the course of a ride, a route independent of the main drive. A boat house stands by the fish pond and a *bath house*, recently

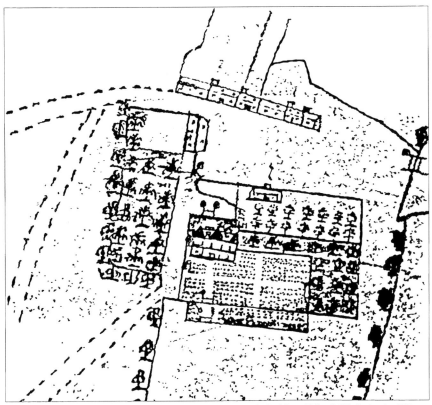

Tracing fom plan of Woolsington Hall dated 1727 by John Robertson. Northumberland Record Office. Bell Collection. Acc.1219.

renovated, is located on the north east of the pond within woodland. Further east in the woodland, is the site of an ice house. Closer to the house, the ha-ha remains in good condition and on the lawn there are some fine mature specimens of cedar, Turkey Oak and Holm Oak. To the east, there is an elegant *orangery* with a rainwater head dated 1797. The large walled garden to the west contains wall trained, goblet trained and espalier fruit trees. The flower gardens contain an early wrought iron rose arbour, arches and trellis work, the beds around the *rosary* are edged with box hedges.

Although Dobson carried out improvements to the house in 1828 there is no evidence that he became involved with the park or gardens. The estate was described in 1825 by Mackenzie, *The mansion house is a neat building, tastefully ornamented with fine plantations. The prospect over this part of the country at the turnpike bar is so extraordinary, that I cannot forbear pointing it out to future ramblers...*

NO PUBLIC ACCESS

Woolsington Hall, Newcastle upon Tyne.

SCOT'S HOUSE — SOUTH TYNESIDE : NZ 327609

Driving east on the Newcastle Road towards Boldon one is aware of a group of imposing trees marking an otherwise unremarkable landscape. The gate-house to Scot's House gives a striking impression of grandeur before one sweeps past. The house was mentioned in Hatfield's survey (1348) and ownership passed through a number of families. In 1617 Thomas Cole surrendered the house to Ralph Cole, the property then passed to the Millbankes and eventually to the Wades by 1800. Described by Mackenzie and Ross in 1834, *Scot's House is a good modern house, sheltered by a grove of trees, near the turnpike road, above one mile west of Boldon.* The 1850s O.S. shows a tantalising outline for what might have been quite a significant garden. West of the pleasure garden, a kitchen garden is annotated with an orchard and glasshouses. Moving east in front of the house a *ha-ha* separated the parkland which was planted with clumps of trees. A path lined with trees crossed the ha-ha to join a route to an observatory, an unusual garden feature. Directly east of the house the pleasure garden appears to have been quartered with three sections containing formal avenues of small trees or shrubs, one is tempted to suggest *topiary*. Perhaps in transition to another style the quarter nearest the drive has been softened with circular paths and a circular island bed surrounded by shrubs. The *ha-ha* was partly obscured by densely planted coniferous and deciduous trees, also suggesting a changeover to another style. Today the garden remains sheltered by a high eighteenth century wall along the north and east sides. The large ornamental pond is derelict and the observatory is barely evident.

NO PUBLIC ACCESS.

OTHER LANDSCAPED PARKS OF INTEREST

FENHAM HALL
NEWCASTLE UPON TYNE : NZ 220654

Now the Convent of the Sacred Heart, mature trees provide a fine context for the buildings. Formerly the park had woodland walks, lawns, individually planted conifers, a fish pond and an ice house. Shown on Gibson's plan of 1788.

NO PUBLIC ACCESS

DUNSTON HILL — GATESHEAD : NZ 220615

The house is a product of a number of phases of eighteenth century building and was the residence for the Carr family. The view of the park from the house is currently obscured by the intrusion of hospital buildings. However, an appreciation of the layout and site of the house can be gained by viewing it from the Team Valley. The park is now used for grazing land but the remains of a ha-ha are evident and magnificent trees are dispersed through the fields. The walled garden is currently being developed with new buildings. The park also once boasted an ice-house and large orchard.

NO PUBLIC ACCESS - VIEWS FROM ADJACENT PUBLIC FOOTPATH.

EPPLETON HALL — SUNDERLAND : NZ 367469

The house is set in extensive gardens facing south west. Many mature trees survive and kitchen garden walls remain at the north west corner of the site.

NO PUBLIC ACCESS

STELLA HALL — GATESHEAD : NZ 175635

Stella Hall stood near the Tyne to the west of Blaydon. The site was a former convent of Benedictine nuns which passed into the hands of the Tempest family in the late sixteenth century. The house was built soon after 1600. The estate was bought by Joseph Cowen in 1850. His son, also Joseph, was a prominent radical politician. He was friendly with many leading European figures of the time and in 1854 entertained Garibaldi, the famous Italian patriot, when he visited Tyneside. Stella Hall was gifted to the University of Durham in 1946, demolished in 1953 and replaced by a suburban housing estate. The Hall was set within a small country estate, and remnants of the landscape can be traced today. A lodge, gardener's house, a bath house, an impressive estate wall and surviving tree planting are all clues to the history of the site. Most impressive though, is the remains of the eighteenth century brick summerhouse, prominent on a hill top, commanding a spectacular view of the Tyne. Here, by local legend Garibaldi pondered his fate. A statue of the great man stood nearby for many years.

LIMITED ACCESS BY PUBLIC FOOTPATH.

C E M E T E R I E S

The swift rise in population which accompanied the industrial expansion of the early nineteenth century drew on town resources heavily. It was acknowledged that the environment was in need of radical adjustment in order to eliminate the harbouring of unhealthy conditions. Corporations were alarmed by the grim consequences of the overcrowded burial grounds in churchyards. Increasingly shallow graves were plundered by vandals and threatened by the spectre of body snatchers. Water courses which ran nearby risked contamination from the prevalent diseases which raged through towns. The problem was similar in France and churchyard burial was banned in Paris in 1804. In Britain it was not until 1853 that the Burial Act gave local authorities the power to close churchyards which had become full. The religious minorities lobbied for public burial grounds as they were limited to the funeral services of established churches. By 1820 non denominational cemeteries appeared in Britain; a particular influence on cemeteries in the north east. Methodism has long been a powerful force for religious thought in the region and other dissenting bodies such as the Presbyterians, Baptists, Quakers and Unitarians were active during this period of intense religious enthusiasm. The numerous churches and chapels in our towns and villages which were built or embellished during the nineteenth century are evidence of this.

Cemeteries can be viewed as precursors to public parks, with some being used as informal open space before the first municipal parks. In the United States the notion was taken further and cemeteries fulfilled a role as pleasure grounds. In accordance with the concern for providing adequate open space for the people of South Shields the Health Committee were instructed to obtain a site for a recreation ground in December 1855. The committee however, reported that they did not recommend any site, because the Bents and sea were already opened to the public *while the new cemetery of 16 acres, with a view of the sea, affords a quiet and pleasing retreat most conducive to health.*

The initial style favoured for the design of cemeteries in Britain was similar to informal landscape parks, a style derived from Parisian influence. When churchyard burial was banned in Paris, Alexandre-Theodore Brongniart designed a cemetery at Père-Lachaise in 1807, a site chosen in a rural location. The concept used for his design was adopted worldwide, bearing the *garden cemetery* ideals. Brongniart used formal avenues leading into winding paths, with trees and shrubs planted in naturalistic groups. The notion of burial in a private pleasure ground was highly attractive to the aspiring members of society who wished to emulate the great and the good. Bowes' fabulous mausoleum at Gibside is a wonderful example of the ascension to immortality from a pleasure ground.

The parkland concept was modified by John Claudius Loudon (1783-1843) who appeared to assume responsibility for all aspects of landscape design in his numerous publications. In *On Laying Out of Cemeteries (1843)* he advised on depths for interment of coffins. He also initiated the notion of cemeteries as venues for education and his practical solution to the security of graves was the provision of lodges to house caretakers. Loudon was opposed to the idea of aping the landscape park. He invoked a style adapted to the sombre requirements of the setting. Cemeteries laid out in the 1820s and 1830s were planted with trees associated with landscaped gardens and the scattered effect was disdained by Loudon as he began to question the picturesque style. He evolved a principle of beauty based on symmetry. His designs were tightly organised visual relationships; man's hand was evident, not hidden, in contrast to the informal landscape park style. Loudon was keen to plant evergreens for both symbolic and practical reasons (as there were no leaves to be raked in autumn). During the height of Loudon's career many varieties of evergreens were introduced from abroad and made ideal specimen trees such as deodar cedar, cypress, juniper, spruce, complementing the traditional English churchyard tree, the yew. Varieties with a weeping habit were also chosen, particularly weeping elm and ash. Loudon also specified deciduous shrubs, bulbs and herbaceous plants although he was most specific about where they should be planted and insisted that they should not give the impression of flower borders; coffin or grave shaped beds were stipulated!

Before the Burial Act was invoked in 1853, new cemeteries were built through commercial ventures and situated on the outskirts of the towns, such as, Newcastle General Cemetery Company who published their prospectus for shareholders in 1834. Once the Burial Act had been established Newcastle City issued an order in 1854 banning further interments in city churchyards. In response All Saint's Cemetery in Jesmond Road was built in 1853, St. John's in Elswick Road was built in 1856, St. Andrew's in Tankerville Terrace established in 1857 and St. Nicholas' in Nun's Moor Road was also built in 1857. The cemeteries run as private companies were fired by the incentive to attract wealthy clients in the hope that their imposing monuments positioned in the most prominent places would attract further clients. When Burial Boards were introduced in 1853 and municipal cemeteries developed, cemetery design evolved into a new phase using starker geometric designs. The increase in urban population, with a predominance of poorer families, meant that the requirement for low cost burials increased whereas the requirement for grand cemeteries declined. Burial Clubs such as the Collecting Society and Commercial Society expanded from the Friendly Societies and were subsequently taken over by insurance companies. These societies were expensive but nevertheless alleviated the terror of a pauper's burial.

By 1870 the American park cemetery approach was further publicised and a reaction to Loudon's dictums ensued. Colourful bedding and deciduous trees were introduced and the paths became informal once again. Jarrow and Monkton Burial Board had an agreement with their superintendent Mr. Ramsay at Jarrow Cemetery allowing him to supply plants for beds, borders and graves using their conservatory. He grew plants with bright colours such as, geranium, viola, calceolaria, echeveria and sedum.

There has been little development in style of cemeteries in the north east since these times. **Whitley Bay Cemetery Chapel** was built in 1913 by Morton in the Arts and Craft style. The cemetery itself is laid out formally with privet hedges and small trees along the paths. A more recent twentieth century cemetery at **Seaton Burn** has a strong utilitarian feeling, emphasised by the flat landscape and lack of embellishment to the design. There are few purpose built crematoria in the county, instead they are usually incorporated into existing cemeteries with little impact on the overall layout.

WESTGATE HILL OR ARTHUR'S HILL CEMETERY
NEWCASTLE UPON TYNE : NZ 237642

This early cemetery was laid out in 1829, providing 3 acres of unconsecrated ground. The people who used the cemetery were of dissenting faiths, some groups had previously carried out burials on the ballast hills below Byker. Scottish Presbyterian immigrants had supposedly started the tradition in their aversion to Anglicanism and had to petition for permission to enclose the fields of graves in 1785 as houses were built close by and ashes from the glassworks heaped there. The Westgate Hill Cemetery Company was formed in 1825. The grounds were laid out and planted in an ornamental style described by Whellan in 1855 as being of similar style to Père-Lachaise in Paris. Reid's map of 1887 shows a modest design with a chapel on an island created by the circular drive which is centred on the entrance off Westgate Road. A wide drive follows the triangular shape of the grounds, also cutting across the centre towards the south east corner. An interesting remnant of the design is evidence of the ground having been deliberately mounded. Today the chapel and perimeter path have gone, and the cemetery is subject to frequent depredations from vandals. There are many trees, although not necessarily original stock, and a number of weeping elms at the western end which are currently suffering from Dutch Elm Disease.

PUBLIC ACCESS

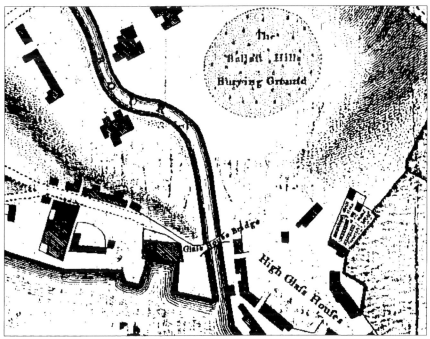

Hutton's plan of Newcastle upon Tyne 1772, showing the Ballast Hill Burial Ground.

NEWCASTLE GENERAL CEMETERY ❖
NEWCASTLE UPON TYNE : NZ 255655

This cemetery was also developed on a triangular site. Newcastle General Cemetery Company was formed in 1834 and commissioned John Dobson to design the buildings which comprise two chapels at the north end, by Jesmond Road. Under each chapel a mortuary vault was provided, solving the problem of storing the coffins before burial at a time of concern for hygiene in the city. Dobson designed colossal gate piers at the entrance from Sandyford Road where a **lodge** was also built. The cemetery is surrounded by a two and a half metre high wall and is located opposite All Saints Cemetery which was built in 1853. The main drive runs through the centre of the site from north-east to south-west and a walk runs parallel to the north wall. The cemetery has two informal areas of open space both given seclusion by groves of trees and shrubs, negotiated by serpentine paths. Loudon was thrilled by Dobson's design and wrote that the entrance would *never be mistaken either for an entrance to a public park or to a country residence.* John Dobson was buried in the cemetery and it is appropriate that he should be surrounded by tributes to an era to which he made such a great contribution. There is an exciting collection of monuments showing the talent of local craftsmen during a period when the city was at a peak of achievement.

LIMITED PUBLIC ACCESS

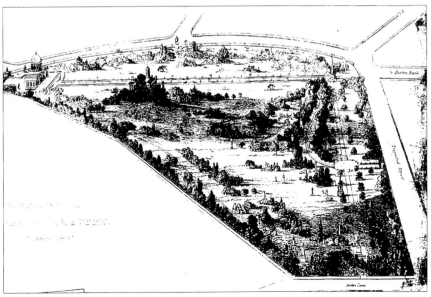

Dobson's proposed view of Newcastle General Cemetery, published with shareholders prospectus 1834.

HARTON CEMETERY — SOUTH TYNESIDE : NZ 376654

Harton has a fine cemetery near Westoe village which was consecrated in 1890. The land comprising of 31 acres was purchased for £300 from the Ecclesiastical Commissioners . By 1894 seventeen acres had been laid out to the designs of Mr. Bernard Cowen. The layout is a simple grid pattern with broad walks and avenues of mature trees. Hodgson described Harton Cemetery in 1924 as *probably one of the handsomest and most tastefully laid out in the north.* The approach to the cemetery gates alongside a plantation of Swedish Whitebeam is striking. The impressive buildings were by Henry Grieves an architect of eclectic style. In the centre of the grounds the two mortuary chapels are linked by an arched gateway with a lantern tower and spire which rises to 103 feet. Monuments line the route to the chapels such as local shipbuilder Robert Readhead's tomb. An area was provided for the burial of members of the Jewish community. The entrance gateway has side gates and the lodge comprises of the superintendent's house and a boardroom for the cemetery committee. The total cost including superintendent's house was £24,488.

PUBLIC ACCESS

Harton Cemetery Chapels.

OTHER CEMETERIES OF INTEREST

There are many cemeteries of interest in the county including the following which all have public access:

ALL SAINT'S CEMETERY
NEWCASTLE UPON TYNE : NZ 258657

St. ANDREWS & JESMOND CEMETERY
NEWCASTLE UPON TYNE : NZ 250662

Both in Jesmond and of a similar layout. All Saint's was consecrated in 1855 and has a very fine specimen elm tree central to the main entrance which is viewed through a gabled Gothic archway designed by *Benjamin Green*. In 1854 the Burial Board of Jesmond merged with St. Andrew to form a joint board. Their cemetery is situated in an unusually tranquil part of Jesmond, further shielded from traffic noise by the handsome remaining trees.

JARROW CEMETERY
SOUTH TYNESIDE : NZ 325645

The Hedworth, Monkton and Jarrow Burial Board was formed in 1864, at a time when the population of Jarrow had increased dramatically because of the success of firms such as Palmers shipyard. Two mortuary chapels were built with brick, one for members of the Church of England and the other for Roman Catholics. The cemetery was consecrated in 1869 by the Bishop of Durham. Six acres of the site was allocated for internment of members of the Church of England and the remaining nine were for Roman Catholics and dissenters. The planting in the cemetery has survived well including hollies, elms, oaks, maples, willow, birch and a variegated elm.

PRESTON CEMETERY
NORTH TYNESIDE : NZ 345693

An extensive cemetery which was opened in 1856. The gate piers, wrought iron gates and railings are retained at the entrance where there is also a large lodge. The layout is formal but has a different feeling to many of the cemeteries discussed as there are many large trees among the graves and laurel hedges along the main drives giving a dark and heavy atmosphere.

GATESHEAD EAST CEMETERY
GATESHEAD : NZ 261625

The cemetery was opened on the 16th August 1862. The church of England and non-conformist chapels survive as does the superintendent's large house (bearing the Gateshead crest and the date 1862) and a lodge. It is a large irregularly shaped cemetery on a north facing hill, divided in two by a path which runs up the slope. The eastern section has a simple grid plan of paths with a central circular area. The western section has a similar central circle but a more irregular plan of paths. The most prominent monument is to Mr. Brockett, Mayor of Gateshead in 1839-40 and a major local political force of his day. There is also a monument to 222 cholera victims from an outbreak which lasted from December 1821 to November 1823. There is a small recreation ground to the north of the cemetery and the remains of Victorian drinking fountains can be seen here, by Sunderland Road and on the Old Durham Road boundary of the cemetery.

MEMORIAL GARDENS

Some of Tyne and Wear's smallest and simplest gardens are also amongst its most charming. Small gardens around war memorials, found throughout the area, are an especially poignant group. Three worthy of note are to be found in the Gateshead area. Clara Vale and Stargate Memorial Gardens commemorate the dead of these former pit communities. Both are small triangular enclosures; the Stargate garden sitting next to a group of Durham Aged Miner's Homes. The Birtley garden is more architecturally ambitious; the war memorial is flanked by two pavilions and the whole is laid out in a formal arrangement.

In Sunderland on the east side of Burdon Road stands a memorial to those who were killed during the First World War. The bronze figure c.1925, represents the Angel of Victory. The sculpture is protected by railings and gates with a cross motif. Lighting is provided by four lamp standards of the same date.

A chilling reminder of the reality of war can be found in the grounds of St. Thomas Churchyard, Barras Bridge, Newcastle. The sculpture by Sir W. Goscombe - John R.A. consists of a series of life size bronze figures of soldiers marching with women and children following, bidding farewell, while above the heads of the men an angel blows a trumpet. The back of the statue has carvings of soldiers in seventeenth and nineteenth century battledress, dated 1694 and 1919, with an inscription commemorating the Northumberland Fusiliers.

PUBLIC ACCESS

Birtley War Memorial, Gateshead.

First World War Memorial by Sir W. Gascombe-John R.A.
St. Thomas Churchyard, Barras Bridge.

MUNICIPAL PARKS

The salvation of green space was not available for town dwellers early in the nineteenth century. In 1833 a report was made to parliament by the Select Committee on Public Walks, following a survey of space accessible to the public in England. The park movement grew bolstered by a deepening concern for the health of the inhabitants of over-crowded industrial towns. Today, with the forethought of our modern planning laws, it is difficult to imagine the chaos and neglect which accompanied the rapid Victorian development of towns; the north east was particularly notorious. The boroughs lacked experience of dealing with problems of such immense proportions and the conditions eventually threatened to discredit the government. In 1842 Chadwick published the *Report on an Inquiry into the Sanitary Condition of the Labouring Population of Great Britain* but it was not until 1848 that the Public Health Act was passed. The first major Public Park was by Paxton at Birkenhead in 1843.

With an avid interest in social reform the Victorians were very keen to provide facilities which attended to both the spiritual and physical requirements of the population and parks offered an ideal solution. When Dr. Hodgkin gave Hodgkin Park to the people of Benwell in 1899, the gift was made without restrictions except that *strong drink shall not be sold in the park.* They were spurred on by the zealous writings of the garden designer Loudon, who

Heaton Park, Newcastle upon Tyne.

thought parks should provide fresh air and offer intellectual stimulation to the working classes. As shorter working hours came into being much thought was given to appropriate leisure pursuits. Activities such as brass band concerts, quoits, and cricket were advocated to draw the public into the parks. Military drilling was popular but fairs, protest meetings and horse racing were not encouraged once parks had been enclosed by the councils. However, these activities were continued at Windmill Hills, in Gateshead, by the rebellious locals despite enclosure in 1861. Pastimes considered suitable for women were encouraged such as skipping, archery, croquet, hockey, tennis and cycling. Sport provided an opportunity for women seeking emancipation to question the imposition of the physical constraints thought befitting for their sex. Children were offered the educational opportunities of viewing caged birds and animals, given sandpits, paddling pools and their play was directed into organised games. The park was a place to wear *Sunday Best* both as clothing and in demeanour. A persistent worry for the middle classes was that they may be offended by the uncouth behaviour of other users of the park and the only way to keep this danger at bay was to draw up copious rules such as no dancing, laundry, shooting or even swimming in some cases. Some of the drinking fountains were inscribed *Keep The Pavement Dry*, such as one in Mowbray Park, Sunderland. The park keepers were constantly employed carrying out maintenance, watching over visitors and guarding the park at night. They often provided a target for mischievious folk intent on provoking them.

The most important feature of parks was and often still remains the floral displays. The designs have changed little since Paxton devised the experience of viewing flower beds from a path. The style of *carpet bedding* evolved; dense mats of coloured plants, often dwarfed varieties, were arranged in complex patterns. With the typical energy of the time the enthusiasts proceeded to debate the subject of colour and arrangement of flower beds throughout the nineteenth century. As more plants were introduced from abroad the urge to display them to their advantage increased. The embroideries of colour previously restricted to *parterres* for grand houses were introduced as bright swirling patterns for all to enjoy. The potential for illustration was realised and commemorative displays were soon emblazoned across the country; this tradition continues and can be viewed in many of the county's parks.

One influence on the popularity of floral displays was the problem posed by pollution. Coal burning killed off mature trees rapidly, as they did not have the vigour to withstand the damage caused by soot. Ash, sycamore, whitebeam became the stalwart trees chosen for their resistance.

Today Victorian Municipal Parks form the backbone of our urban parks, many retaining original layouts and features. These parks offer a tableau of local history whether commemorating the gift of land, local heroes and heroines, or victims of wars. A park which has the stamp of local identity gives the locality distinct qualities in contrast to the corporate house styles of organisations which proliferate on our high streets.

LEAZES PARK ❖ — NEWCASTLE UPON TYNE : NZ 242648

Leazes Park is located on the northern limits of Newcastle city centre and provides a contrast with the wide open space of the Town Moor close by. Organising the first purpose built municipal park in the city was a taxing task for the councillors. In 1863 the architect and cartographer Thomas Oliver drew up plans for a formal park which included land across to Brandling Village. The suggestions were not acceptable to the committee and John Hancock, brother of the naturalist Albany Hancock, was then commissioned to produce plans in 1871. Hancock's plan was inspired by eighteenth century landscape park design, disregarding requirements for recreational facilities which was a huge priority at the time. John Laing, who worked previously for Lord Armstrong as a steward, was asked to submit a design for the Castle Leazes, eventually the only area which was developed into a park. Having won the commission he made provision for skating, bowls and croquet. The existing boating lake built in 1872 is the centrepiece of the design. A path leading from the west lodge approaches a stone terrace from which views across the park are framed by a stone balustrade. In 1991 the City Council held a national competition for the renewal of Leazes Park but no improvements have as yet followed.

PUBLIC ACCESS

JESMOND DENE ❖ — INCORPORATING ARMSTRONG PARK & HEATON PARK : NEWCASTLE UPON TYNE : NZ 263665

This extremely popular park winds along a deep dene following the Ouseburn for almost 1.5 miles. The slopes of the dene are densely wooded with a profusion of evergreen trees and shrubs, including cedars, junipers, Californian Redwoods, varieties of yew and holly and the ubiquitous rhododendron beloved of the Victorians. A great variety of deciduous trees were also planted including elm, beech, oak, cherry and poplars. The dene was originally laid out in relation to Jesmond Towers, the home of Lord Armstrong who donated the park to Newcastle Corporation in 1883. The house was enlarged by John Dobson in 1820 who also built a banqueting house in 1860. There are many other architectural features; a lodge by Norman Shaw 1870, Armstrong Bridge 1879, St. Mary's Chapel - a medieval building supposedly frequented by pilgrims, St. Mary's holy well with eighteenth or early nineteenth century stonework and an eighteenth century water mill. The mill was retained by Armstrong as a feature above the gorge which he designed.

Heaton Park and Armstrong Park were combined with Jesmond Dene when Armstrong Park was opened in 1884 by the Prince and Princess of Wales. Charleton describes the *'beautiful pieces of old woodland, which have for generations been left for the most part in Nature's hands'*. Although he accepted the need for the laying out of walks Charleton was affronted by the designer Mr. Fowler's ideas, *the digging up of soil by the sides of more secluded footpaths, and the wild underwood which was originally there. We fancy that ferns and brambles, primroses and bluebells, growing in rich profusion as nature alone can arrange them, are better objects to look at by the side of a woodland path than rhododendrons and such like plants, stuck in formal array in the naked soil, with a border of broken stones and London Pride.* Heaton Park was once part of Heaton estate which belonged to the Ridley family. The park served a large area of terraced housing which stretched east to a mass of railway sidings and south to industrial buildings along the River Tyne. This section of the park sloped down wooded banks to a large field. Close to the east entrance a temple - like building was constructed for Sir Mathew White Ridley which was presented by his tenants and admirers. To the north, stand the ruins of a medieval building - the *Camera* or chamber of Adam de Jesmond. In 1887 Bulmer described the park and mentioned various livestock, an eagle, a racoon, several monkeys and a bear pit which was sunk by the lake.

PUBLIC ACCESS

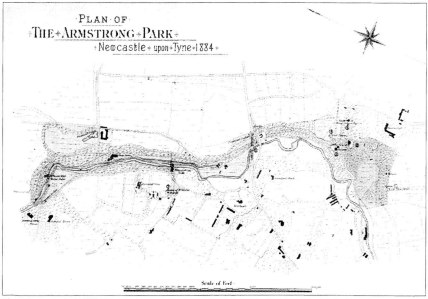

Plan of Armstrong Park, 1884.

MOWBRAY PARK — SUNDERLAND : NZ 398565

Sunderland Corporation applied to the government in 1840 for a grant to develop a public park on the site of Building Hill and were awarded £750. Originally given the democratic name of People's Park, Mowbray Park was laid out by Mr Lawson, gardener to Lord Londonderry who previously also worked at Seaham Hall. He was assisted by Joseph Smith who had worked at Chatsworth and was perhaps influenced by Paxton, the head gardener there from 1826. Their approach was to partially level the site retaining the hill around which winding paths were incorporated providing views of the town. There was little planting apart from individual trees; the designers must have appreciated that the open views were a priority. Later, land was identified north of the railway line as being suitable for an extension of the park. After a lengthy debate, questioning the lavish cost of the proposals, the land was purchased and a competition was held for a suitable design. Despite 30 submissions for schemes, Mr. James Lindsay, who had not entered the competition was commissioned to do the work. He provided a lake, terrace and mounds on the previously level surface. Despite further concerns that the lake would become stagnant, the park was opened on 10th July 1866. The town was given a half days holiday where along with 17,000 adults and children, civic dignitaries, Durham Regiments and bands proceeded from the east end of Sunderland to the park.

MARINE PARKS — SOUTH TYNESIDE : NZ 371674

Having achieved the status of County Borough the Corporation of South Shields was quick to initiate the building of parks for the benefit of the population. However, the Ecclesiastical Commissioners were unhurried in providing a site and after protracted negotiations a former brickyard was chosen. The Earl of Chichester visited the town as Chairman of the Board of Ecclesiastical Commissioners, having been asked to investigate provision of open space, and he recommended that further tracts of land should be made available for recreational use. South Shields Corporation employed Mathew Hall, Borough Engineer and Surveyor to lay out the north park. Work began in 1883 and was completed in 1890 at a total cost of £20,000.

Municipal Park design was not a subject which inspired Victorian horticultural writers, gardening journals tended to focus on private gardens. However, the *Gardener's Calendar*

Park and Ballast Hills, South Shields.

chose to single out the Marine Parks and praise the scheme in 1886; they thought the park imparted *volumes for the taste and skill of Mr Mathew Hall as he had transformed the barren waste into a landscape which will form a most healthful ornament to the town when the southern half, just commenced, has been completed.* The ballast hills to the north were planted up and terraces were cut into the slope giving generous views of the sea. The walks and terraces were constructed with red ash. On the west side a 50 foot wide carriage - drive was constructed, as traditionally park visitors often rode in a carriage to take air. The eastern side of the park was protected by a concrete battlemented wall. A gardener's lodge was built at the entrance on Park Terrace Road. The central feature of the park was an ornamental bandstand encircled by a 30 foot wide gravel walk. The rockeries were praised by the *Gardener's Calendar* and even the large numbers of neatly designed, comfortable seats were mentioned. Mathew Hall planted trees, shrubs and hardy perennial borders densely. There was great scepticism as to whether any plants would grow in such hostile coastal weather conditions but the planting flourished. No doubt through the wisdom of dense planting and judicious choice of plant material. The Shields Gazette listed Ontario poplar, golden and common elder, sycamore, Huntingdon willow, oval leaved privet, and flowering currant.

South Marine Park was designed on a grander scale. The dominant feature was a lake for sailing model boats; this idea was vehemently opposed but proved to be very popular. A circular drive connected the park with a new road under construction by the Commisioners and a road being laid out by the Harton Coal Company. During the 1890s the town suffered greatly from the effects of depression in trade and the borough were able to employ 200 men to level the ballast and build South Marine Park.

PUBLIC ACCESS

ROKER PARK — SUNDERLAND : NZ 406590

The park was built within a ravine, Roker Gill, which leads down to the beach at Roker Rocks. The land for Roker Park was presented jointly to the town by the Hedworth Williamson family and the Ecclesiastical Commissioners in an effort to upgrade the surrounding area and encourage house building. A condition of the gift was that a road bridge was built spanning the valley, providing access to land further afield enabling expansion of quality housing in Roker. As Hendon Valley, Valley Gardens and Victoria Gardens had been developed for housing, Roker Dene was one of the few green spaces available in Sunderland for recreation. Hendon Valley contained beech trees and a profusion of wild flowers and in the nineteenth century was called the Valley of Love. The valley was a popular venue to watch balloon ascents and tight-rope exhibitions. The seaside provided a vital connection between health and holidays and Roker served as an important resort. The 'ozone' was thought to be beneficial and sea bathing was promoted. People came from the countryside as well as the towns to take the sea air often travelling by the extensive rail network which existed at the time.

The layout of Roker Park was fairly simple. A belt of trees and shrubs were planted around the boundary ensuring that the visitors attention was not distracted by features outside the park. The trees also provided shade, an important requirement as the Victorians shunned direct sunlight - hence the vital accessory of a parasol. The bandstand, dated 1880, is positioned on a small promontory looking out to sea. The characteristic shape of bandstands was influenced originally by Chinese style garden buildings which were popular in Europe in the middle of the eighteenth century. Brass band music was an intrinsic part of Victorian park recreation and bandstands became a popular attraction. On the highest point of the park an Anglican cross of 1904 stands as a memorial to The Venerable Bede, the monk and scholar who wrote *The Ecclesiastical History of the English People* in 731 and worked in the monasteries at Jarrow and Monkwearmouth. The space around the boating lake is broken up into lawns divided by shrubs and trees, intersected by serpentine paths. A drinking fountain was installed by the lake to commemorate the opening of the park and Centenary of the Sunday Schools in 1880. At the northern end, the bowling green was completed in 1902.

The sides of the dene were softened with shrub planting and in one spot a small waterfall features in a grotto. The descent into the dene is the beginning of a drama with a conclusion that the local painter John Martin (1789-1854) would have appreciated. His paintings depicted humanity dwarfed to insignificance by the landscape. A similar experience can be gained at the end of the winding path when the visitor confronts the roaring German Ocean, as it was then called. The seaside promenades were built during the recession of 1885-6 and provided work for an employment scheme.

PUBLIC ACCESS

Bandstand, Roker Park, Sunderland.

NORTHUMBERLAND PARK — NORTH TYNESIDE : NZ 362691

During the recession of the 1880s the Tynemouth alderman, John Foster-Spence approached the Duke of Northumberland requesting a piece of land suitable for a park. His ambition was to provide work for unemployed shipbuilders and a facility for the town. Northumberland Park was opened in 1885 by the Duke of Northumberland who planted a Turkey Oak, one of many commemorative trees subsequently planted in the park. The park was designed by Mr. Gomozinski the Borough Surveyor. The following delightful, but excitable, description was written in a brochure produced by Tynemouth and North Shields Corporation in 1923, *The phrase, "a perfect paradise", may be somewhat hackneyed, but it is at least accurate when applied to this delightful resort. A long valley through which a tiny burn flowed at it's own sweet will has been transformed into a veritable "garden of the Lord". Here are shady trees, rustic bridges, tasteful flower beds, smooth patches of turf, fragrant shrubs, well kept paths, banks on whose sides are a mass of colour in the spring and summer, cosy arbours, pretty ornamental lakes on which wild fowl and graceful swans disport themselves, and last, though by no means least, a plentiful supply of seats. There are a number of bowling greens, and band performances frequently add to the many floral and sylvan attractions of this sweet spot.* There was great civic pride in the park - While most benefactors found waterfowl and swans appropriate gifts for the town park, one councillor in 1897 was moved to offer an alligator for the lake!

PUBLIC ACCESS

Northumberland Park, North Shields.

SALTWELL PARK — GATESHEAD : NZ 255610

Saltwell Park is probably the finest traditional municipal park in the north east. It remains a very popular traditional park with excellent bedding displays, bowls, boating, events and well used areas for informal recreation. The development of the park was an inspired piece of opportunism. It was superimposed on the estate of the nationally prominent stained glass manufacturer William Wailes, who had built himself a romantic polychromatic villa, Saltwell Towers, together with a complex garden using retaining walls as castellated belvederes. A natural dene was incorporated as a picturesque approach to the house. Shortly after it's construction Wailes fell into financial difficulties, and the estate was purchased by the Corporation in 1876 to form a municipal park. The design for this was undertaken by Edward Kemp. At that time he was the Superintendant of Birkenhead Park, usually cited as the first designed public park in the world. Kemp had worked with the designer of Birkenhead Park, Joseph Paxton, and was a noted designer in his own right.

In the southern section of Saltwell Park Kemp made modest adaptions to Wailes' ambitious garden by enhancing the circulation and skilfully inserting closed spaces for formal games such as bowls and quoits. In the northern section open fields were incorporated as parkland using a more conventional municipal park plan. This area has strong peripheral tree planting and sinuous paths and tree clumps. Along the upper side is a formal promenade broad walk terminated by two rustic shelters and at it's centre a refreshment pavilion with an axial view down to a large irregularly shaped lake. Subsequent changes have included an extension of

Saltwell Park, Gateshead, 1920's

1920 to incorporate Saltwell Grove house and it's garden to the south. A successful addition has been the creation of a beautiful and tranquil rose garden.

Pet's Corner, the aviaries and the wildfowl on the lake are all popular attractions with visitors today. In it's early years the park showed signs of being transformed into a zoo. The main promulgator of this was the Chief Constable of Gateshead whose repeated requests for permission to donate further animals and birds were often turned down by the Parks Committee. Nevertheless in 1880 he successfully contributed aviaries stocked with birds, and in the same year a monkey house. The monkeys were a controversial acquisition as certain aspects of their behaviour gave great cause for concern, somewhat offending Victorian sensibilities. In 1882 Lord Ravensworth presented two deer to the park and it may have been one of these which involved the Corporation in litigation and expenses of £650 when a visitor was gored by a stag. Further trouble occured in 1890 when the park's racoon was presented to London Zoo and it was resolved that in future 'no vicious animal' would be allowed in the park.

PUBLIC ACCESS

WINTER GARDENS

Winter gardens, often called *Peoples Palaces*, were vast glasshouses built on cast iron frames which provided venues for public entertaiment The most famous and influential of these buildings was Paxton's Crystal Palace built in 1850. At **Tynemouth Park** a complex containing an aquarium, winter gardens (called summer gardens in the appropriate months) and skating rink was built by London architects John Norton and Philip E. Masey. The company dissolved in 1877 and the building became a theatre. At **Mowbray Park** a Winter garden was built in the Extension Park alongside the Library and Museum. The building contained a collection of exotic plants, ferns, birds and fish. As with many such buildings it was bombed in 1941 and demolished in 1942.

PRIVATE PARKS & GARDENS

Access to private parks was restricted to key holders who lived in surrounding terraces. **Percy Gardens** in Tynemouth was created by the residents of the crescent which stood to the rear. The houses had not been provided with gardens and it was assumed a park nearby would meet requirements. The park has an elegant simplicity, built around an eliptical shape. The outer edge was laid out using banks to provide shelter on the east side, the seaward face. Paths leading in from the houses follow serpentine routes to a circular path in the centre. In 1872 plans for a gardener's cottage were approved and a lodge built at the southern end.

Portland Park was on Jesmond Road and opened in July 1874. It covered four acres, with a croquet lawn, bowling green and *lawn tennis grounds.*

Albert Drive Park was opened in 1906 by Alderman Robert Affleck. During his ceremonial speech he commented on the provision of the park as part of the development, adding that the local community should not be dependent upon municipal resources.

Albert Drive Park, Gateshead.

OTHER PARKS OF INTEREST

FELLING PARK — GATESHEAD : NZ 275620

Felling Park was opened in July 1910, wrapping round the impressive Felling Town Hall which had been built in 1902. This small park is now best known for consistently providing spectacular displays of bedding plants. These are very prominent on the slope which rises from Sunderland Road. Above this there is a more informal grass area, fringed by trees and with an open bandstand at the centre. Formal sports were situated on either side of the core of the park: a bowling green on one side, tennis courts on the other. Above the bowling green is a small rockery area with rustic stonework. The original park was later extended to the west.

CARR-ELLISON PARK — SOUTH TYNESIDE : NZ 315643

The park was gifted to the community in 1897 by the Carr-Ellison family and in 1920 Colonel Carr-Ellison gave a memorial to *Hebburn men who laid down their lives in the service of their country and as a token of gratitude for the safe return of his only son, John Campbell Carr-Ellison, Lieutenant 1st Royal Dragoons.*

The park was built in the grounds of Hebburn Hall which was gentrified c.1790 and altered by Dobson in 1819. The hall had a very large walled garden to the west. The Carrs and Ellisons were great gardeners and when Carr moved to Cheshire c.1740 he wrote a letter concerning gardening and mentioned the *Ashton* pear which he had discovered and was sending to be planted at Hebburn. *I think it so delicate a melting pear that if it equal'd the Beurre in size it might very well rival it.*

Today the park has an open aspect to the south. An intriguing dell is sheltered by woodland to the north and on the north west side bowling greens dominate the grounds.

BARNES PARK — SUNDERLAND : NZ 375555

Opened in 1909 it is a small park which is bisected by the Durham Road. The name of the park was taken from the Bishopwearmouth Burn which flowed through the fields. The burn runs along the valley in the park to the lake with surplus water forming a small waterfall at the end of the lake. The 33 acres of land were purchased in 1904 for £8,500. During the depression of trade the park provided work for the unemployed. In addition to the gardeners, 2,798 men were employed to build the park. Trees already growing on the site were retained to complement the oak, ash, beech and elm, which were planted -many of which are now reaching maturity. The lake and the bandstand have survived, the latter listed Grade II.

READHEAD PARK BOROUGH OF SOUTH TYNESIDE : NZ 374656

In May 1923 the Robert Readhead Park was opened after Alderman Readhead gave the land in thanksgiving for peace. The gift was conditional as Readhead stipulated that unemployed ex-servicemen should be employed building roads nearby. This was another contentious choice as a site for a park as other local councillors stood to benefit from the Corporation building houses on the land but they were substantially outvoted.

ELSWICK PARK
NEWCASTLE UPON TYNE : NZ 232636

In 1878 Elswick Hall was purchased by the Corporation who used the hall to display sculpture by John Graham Lough and Matthew Noble, both distinguished sculptors. Mr. A.M. Fowler laid out an ornamental lake, croquet lawn, walks, lodges, fencing and other features. In 1981 an innovative swimming pool was built in the park as part of a scheme designed by Napper Collerton Partnership.

The Lake, Elswick Park, Newcastle upon Tyne

VILLA   GARDENS

The first villas in the county include Ryton Grove at Ryton built in c.1742 and West Hendon House, Sunderland c.1800. These were scaled down versions of the country houses and parks owned by the nobility. Possession of the countryside by the land owning classes signified status and power and the newly prosperous merchants aspired to emulate their peers. Villas with large gardens increased in number as agricultural returns diminished and the newer landowners wanted estates without managerial or financial problems; small country estates without the encumbrance.

During the nineteenth century the villa changed in style from an elite extravagant building to merely a large house designed to echo the qualities of the original villas. Perhaps eroneously included amongst this category are houses called Villas by their architects which were little more than grand suburban houses with a typical garden measuring a quarter of an acre. The ambitions resting on these houses were high and prosperity gained from industry was put to careful use to indicate the position of the resident household in society. Victorian architecture revelled in a eclectic range of styles and as the industrialists built their villas on the outskirts of towns their architects enthusiastically fashioned Classical, Italianate, Gothic and other styles to suit every taste. In some areas we see a nucleus of villas remaining such as in Low Fell, Gateshead and Ashbrooke, Sunderland; while other groups have been obliterated or surrounded by later building development such as Willington Villa, Ropery Lane, North Tyneside where the only remaining trace is a short stretch of the southern boundary wall and original trees on the western boundary.

Away from the noise and worst pollution emanating from industrial sites, villa society set about adding further enchantment to the distance. Few things must have delighted them more than the surfeit of horticultural consumerism offered by new plants and trees, equipment, books, magazines, and buildings. Even moral expedience was available! Shirley Hibberd wrote in *Rustic Adornment* (1856) *A home of taste is a tasteful home, wherein everything is a reflection of refined thoughts and chaste desires .... In such a home Beauty presides over the education of the Sentiments and while the intellect is ripened by the many means which exist for the acquisition of knowledge, the moral nature is refined by those silent appeals of Nature and of Art, which are the foundation of Taste.* The romance of the garden inspired the use of flowers and leaves as motifs which were incorporated into numerous patterns for domestic ornamentation on material, wallpaper, plaster relief work, china, etc.

Innumerable debates questioned the nature of appropriate taste in horticulture. Loudon led a rebellion against the *Picturesque* by using unusual exotic plants arranged to display their beauty to the greatest advantage. Loudon's *Gardenesque* principles were published in his books, notably *The Suburban Gardener* and *Villa Companion* (1838) and his magazine *The Gardener's Magazine*. Horticultural writers gave householders the freedom to create their own gardens, alleviating them from tyranny imposed by designers, nurserymen, or gardeners.

Introduction of exotic plant material increased dramatically during the early 1800s. Many of the tender plants such as lillies and orchids were displayed in conservatories which were a vital adjunct to any worthy house. Ferns were a passionate interest at the time and were grown in collections called *Ferneries* outside in the garden, while tender introductions from abroad were grown in conservatories. *Beeton's Dictionary of Gardening* (c.1880) extols the virtues of the fern and advises readers to consult nurserymens' catalogues to make their choices *where they will find ample information on the subject, and to visit their nurseries where they will see such specimens as may provoke envy without doing harm.* The design of the garden was centred around plants themselves rather than plants being used as a palette to illustrate the design.

Whereas the passer-by was often permitted to view an eighteenth century landscaped park, the Victorians sought privacy and only the towers of a Victorian villa would be visible, rising above the fringe of impenetrable woodland planting. The use of plants with dark glossy leaves such as laurel, rhododendrons, hollies, made a backdrop for specimen trees, shrubs and flower beds packed with gaudy blocks of coloured annual plants. The nineteenth century was an era of novelty and delight was taken in having numerous species. Botanical interest was often more important than the relationships between the plants as groups. Later, William Robinson and Gertrude Jeykll were able to demonstrate the benefit of subtle relationships between colour and form.

Conservatory leading from dwelling-house- Shirley Hibberd 1856.

Once the passion for revivalist styles of architecture began in the 1820s the garden revivalists began to implement their responses and a period of confusion ensued for those who did not adhere to Loudon's principles. Twenty years later the wide open landscape and classical references had been discarded in favour of influences from seventeenth century *parterres* and gardens of the Italian Renaissance which the designer Charles Barry (1795-1860) found inspirational. William Andrew Nesfield was born in Chester le Street (1793-1881). His career developed during the 1830s when he began working with architects who had adopted medieval and English Renaissance styles; one of the architects, Anthony Salvin was also from County Durham. Nesfield's designs returned to the formality of parterres using seventeenth century designs and he also incorporated monograms. He worked throughout the country, frequently in Yorkshire and Cumberland. Regrettably his only commissions in the north east were at Alnwick Castle, Northumberland, and Upleatham Hall, Cleveland. Nesfield's work has not survived well as many English country houses suffered a long and lingering decline due to economic pressures and labour intensive garden features were early casualties.

John Dobson the doyen of architecture in the north east referred to himself as an architect and landscape gardener. Dobson's father was a publican at The Pineapple, Chirton, North Shields, he also kept a nursery, a common sideline for publicans at that time. Dobson was a sensitive plantsman and this is illustrated by an affidavit which he wrote in 1849 explaining his design principles for a plantation at Bolam (1816). Dobson appreciated the requirements for tree plantations to fulfil visual potential but he also designed with good husbandry in mind for profitable timber. Few of his designs specify landscape design work although they show evidence of his interest in the subject such as Jesmond General Cemetery.

A style which has delighted gardeners and garden observers for a century was generated by the gardening writer William Robinson (1838-1935) who wrote *The Wild Garden* in 1870 and Gertrude Jekyll a painter, writer and designer. Jekyll's book *Wood and Garden*, published in 1899, developed Robinson's ideas leading a movement away from rigid designs planted with garishly coloured plants and pleaded for subtlety in both colour and form. Her friendship with Edwin Lutyens led them to collaborate on designs for houses and gardens throughout the country. Although they worked at Lindisfarne Castle and Blagdon, no examples have come to light in Tyne and Wear. The essence of their gardens lingered and was sustained with the Arts and Craft Movement by designers such as Thomas Mawson the influential landscape designer, who worked from the Lake District. Because Jekyll's philosophy was based on the principles of cottage gardening, the ideas are well suited to small gardens and interpretations of her work continue today.

ASHBURNE HOUSE — CITY OF SUNDERLAND : NZ 398557

The house was built for Edward Backhouse who was a Quaker and member of a family of bankers and great nurserymen in York. A description of the house was written in *The Journal of Horticulture* in 1878 and provides a detailed insight into a typical villa garden of the time. A wide variety of plant material was used with many supplied from the family nursery. The drive approached the house from the north and was ornamented with standard rhododendrons in tubs. The author was surprised by the condition of the trees as the house was so close to the sea. There were good specimens of beech, elm, sycamore and Turkey Oak. A terraced border in front of the house was divided by diamond shaped beds set on *Cerastium tomentosum* a form of chickweed. The beds were planted with yellow *Calceolaria*, scarlet geraniums, *Viola, Arabis variegata* (rock cress), with a centre of *Coleus Verschaffelti* - a variety with wildly variegated leaves which grew particularly well outside. Borders at the west end of the house were planted with perennials, the centre bed, *the most attractive bed of it's kind we have seen this season*, was planted as follows; a star set in a circle with two central circles holding the piece de resistance a specimen *Echeveria retusa* - a succulent from America, surrounded by *Alternathera amoena* - described by Robinson as *little tropical weeds* from Brazil. *Sedum acre* (stonecrop) provided the groundcover for triangular sections of the star which were planted with a tricolour Pelargonium, *Mrs Pollock*. Other sections were filled with lobelia, pyrethrum, while the bar lines and edge were drawn with *Echevaria secunda lauca*- another variety of the fleshy succulent from America. The conservatory was a significant feature containing an eight foot wide central path and laid with Minton tiles. The warm conditions offered suitable accommodation for the huge collection of plants, some

Ashburne House, Sunderland, 1878.

reaching great heights such as a *Dracaena Veitchii* which grew to 20 feet high. A walk to the pleasure garden led past an elaborate octagonal summerhouse and looked down onto many trees and shrubs, chestnuts, purple beeches, standard rhododendrons in tubs (moved to the conservatory when flowering), evergreen oaks, Aucubas and a collection of thorns. *At the bottom of the incline we take a turn to the left, and the beauty of the place is spread before the eye in all it's loveliness. Over the fountain, throwing it's silvery spray, a good view of the grounds is obtained, to which the artist has done no more than justice in the accompanying engraving.*

The kitchen garden was also a revelation. Through the centre of the garden a series of glasshouses contained an extraordinary number of vines, *Black Hamburg, Golden Hamburg, Black Prince, Grizzly and White Frontignan, Lady Downes, Trebbiano, Black Alicante, Muscat of Alexandria* and Mr. Crament's (the gardener) seedling *Grape Ashburne Seedling.* The second glasshouse was also planted with vines, figs and underplanted with 250 azaleas protected from strong sunlight by a canvas shade. In the *stove* measuring 50 feet by 24 feet vast numbers of decorative plants were grown presumably to be moved to the conservatory or house when flowering. Further buildings contained supplies of Poinsettias, orchids, Peach trees, a Marechal Niel Rose which produced 300 blooms in one season, Pelargoniums, Fuchsias and Begonias.

Much of the land was absorbed into Backhouse Park where little remains of the original garden apart from the fountain filled with plants. Recently the Sunderland Antiquarian Society have arranged for a variety of *Backhouse* daffodils to be planted in the park. William Backhouse (1807-69) bred narcisi at St. John's Hall, Wolsingham in Weardale and made important developments m the breeding of daffodils.

PUBLIC PARK

Design for garden of a quarter of an acre, 1856.

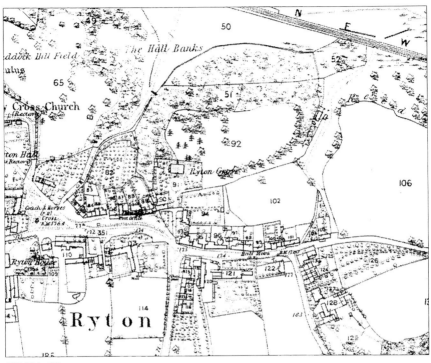

1857 Edition O.S. map

RYTON GROVE — GATESHEAD : NZ 153647

Ryton Grove is a fascinating villa which was built in 1742. The gardens shown on the 1857 O.S. map are intriguing. The house faces south with a turning circle bordered on both sides by trees. On the north front a path leads away into the woodland. On the east side of the house the park dominates the view which extends for several miles along the River Tyne. The park was planted with many individual trees including firs and on the north side deciduous woodland shielded the railway line which dropped into a cutting further east. Powerful landowners were sometimes able to stipulate cuttings for railway lines in order that parkland views were not impeded. The walled garden south east of the house is a gem, box hedges line the paths and many fruit trees remain. A gazebo stands against the east wall and a range of glasshouse stand against the north wall. Although the parkland is under separate ownership the garden is intact although vulnerable through ageing.

NO PUBLIC ACCESS

HEATHFIELD HOUSE — GATESHEAD : NZ 257609

In the second half of the nineteenth century suburban development around the small village of Low Fell south of Gateshead gathered momentum. Much of this consisted of the building of substantial villas for specific clients, mainly wealthy industrialists. In effect the area became the *West End* Newcastle never truly had. These villas were usually set in large grounds and the creation of an impressive garden seems to have been the preoccupation of many of the owners. The three most elaborate gardens were at Saltwell Towers, Whinney House and Heathfield House. The Heathfield garden was developed by German brothers called Lange. The house was placed in the north east corner of the site and the rest was given over to an elaborate garden. The most notable feature was a circular lake at the centre of which was a small circular island on which stood a glass pagoda. A large conservatory was built over a dene and elsewhere an artificial hill was surmounted by a full sized metal eagle. Sadly a proposal in 1896 to include Heathfield as an extension to Saltwell Park never came to pass and the garden was eventually built on for Heathfield School. The house survives, as do the gate piers topped by carved stone lions which form a landmark on Durham Road.

NO PUBLIC ACCESS

Heathfield House, Gateshead, Main entrance gates

WHINNEY HOUSE - GATESHEAD : NZ 255605

Whinney House is the grandest of the Low Fell villas. It is large, solid and of an Italianate design, constructed of beautifully tooled sandstone. It was built for Edward Joicey, an industrialist and coal owner. The house lies at the centre of what, for a suburban area, was a substantial estate of over 30 acres and seems to have been an attempt by Joicey to create a miniature county estate in the town. He purchased the land, with his brother John, in 1864. Work on the construction of Whinney House was begun soon afterwards and took place in a series of stages over the next twenty years or so. The garden design has been credited to Albany Hancock, the famous Newcastle naturalist; although it may have been the work of John Hancock his brother, who was known as a garden designer. The garden incorporates two denes, both of which were bridged. The southern bridge across Whinney House Dene led to St. Helen's Church, a very fine building designed by John Wardle and paid for by Edward Joicey. There is a special door for the family on the north side. One of the most remarkable garden features was a glazed walk which led from a large conservatory, via an eccentric gazebo with views over Whinney House Dene, through to the large kitchen garden. Surviving remnants show this walk incorporated ornamental rustic stonework and a small water cascade. It may have been used as a fernery. Other notable features include a fine fountain, a sunken area at the front of the house which may have been a tennis court or ice rink, stables and a lodge. As with other villas in the area Whinney House made full use of extensive views westward over the Team Valley. Indeed it is orientated so as to give a direct view, framed by garden planting, across the valley to Ravensworth Castle.

NO PUBLIC ACCESS

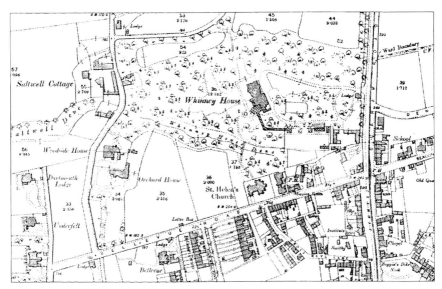

1898 Edition O.S. map

LITTLE BENTON — NEWCASTLE UPON TYNE : NZ 265685

John Dobson produced a volume of estate plans for William Clark, showing land at Cullercoats Little Benton, Monkseaton and New Whitley in 1813. While the drawings are mostly functional, the plan of Little Benton is exquisite and shows Dobson's talent as a draughtsman and visionary. The view to the north front was framed by a plantation with an irregular edge on the west. The northern perimeter of the estate was bounded by further plantations with a grove of trees directly north of the house. A ride followed along the boundary. The view south of the house was directed towards a gap in planting on the south-west by a circular stand of trees perhaps affording a view of Heaton Park and Newcastle in the distance. The southern perimeter plantation constrained any further views to the south.

The walled garden was enormous yet despite this the kitchen garden continued outside the walls, possibly indicating use as an extension of the pleasure grounds.

By the time of the 1896 O.S. map the landscape had been changed dramatically. Little Benton was renamed Benton Park and Benton Hall had been built. The small pond was enlarged into a lake with islands and the tree belt north west of the house was softened by further informal planting. The wooded walk around the kitchen garden was opened up leaving a slender shelter belt on the western edge. North of the house a turning circle was introduced removing the meandering approach. The garden on the south front was extended into the park and a terrace and steps down to the lawns were added. Small clumps of trees were dispersed in the park and the southern perimeter planting was softened by individual trees standing in the park.

SITE BUILT OVER

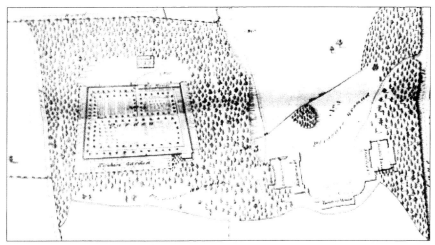

Plan drawn by John Dobson, 1813, for William Clark.

VILLA REAL later NAZARETH HOUSE
NEWCASTLE UPON TYNE : NZ 265655

The house on Sandyford Road was built by Dobson in 1817 for Captain Dutton. Dobson's plan gives a fascinating insight into a design for a villa on the outskirts of a large town at that time. The grounds comprising of just over twenty one acres were extensively landscaped in Dobson's style and orientated towards the south. At the entrance from Sandyford Road a lodge overlooks wide, curved lawns edged with woodland. The carriage drive intersected winding woodland walks directed towards glasshouses to the north-west. The residents were well provided for with two *pineries* and two *vinery* sheds, behind which, a chimney stood in woodland. East of the house a vast walled garden is shown with trees planted along the routes of the paths. On the western wall two curved walls are drawn forming a shelter with a view across the garden. In the centre a cistern has stones heaped around the base. Further east an extensive melon ground is drawn. Melons were grown in frames with the soil lower than ground level. Paths lead from the walled garden out into the parkland and towards a pond complete with fishing house. Wide views from the house led to small groves of trees and sections of dense planting with further clumps located in the park beyond. The house was located on a terrace which sloped down to the lawn. Villa Real is now a convent and the grounds have been reduced on the east side due to housing development. Gardens on the south and west side remain.

NO PUBLIC ACCESS

BACKWORTH HOUSE now THE MINERS' WELFARE HALL
— NORTH TYNESIDE : NZ 302717

The hall was built by William Newton between 1778 - 1780 and is within a conservation area. Despite the loss of peripheral embellishments to the house and alterations to the rear it is still an attractive building. The house was adapted for recreational use c.1940 and a golf course has been built in the grounds. The boundaries are undisturbed and much of the original planting is evident. The boundary wall remains and there are remnants of outbuildings. The kitchen garden is disused.

LIMITED PUBLIC ACCESS

PLANNED
DEVELOPMENTS

A unified approach to housing developments began as large scale schemes were built. As contruction was organised by individual companies it was inevitable their approach would show characteristic features. **Northumberland Square** in North Tyneside, where the earliest terrace was built in 1810, and **Charlotte Square** where the first terrace was built in 1770, have the elegance of London Squares which was perhaps the selling point of the buildings and subsequent development.

Council housing began after the First World War and planned estates signalled a new approach to community housing, This century has witnessed incredible changes and at the same time provided considerable opportunities to experiment with design. Architects have been given the freedom to use concepts interwoven with many disciplines and aided by progress in technology.

Cedars Green in Gateshead is a small prestigious development of local authority housing and was built in 1954 just before the first high rise developments in the country. It comprises of 59 houses of a variety of designs. The estate is set back from the former A1 and laid out in an informal style with many of the houses facing a central green. It was developed in the grounds of The Cedars, an Italiaenate Victorian villa of c.1874.

Bog House, Gateshead was built during the late 1920s in the *garden suburb* style. The aim of such developments was to create housing which would accommodate a mixed community. In order to provide an intimate atmosphere small village like streets were built with grass verges alongside, planted with trees. **The Spinney** in High Heaton, Newcastle, is an inter-war estate constructed using radiating semi circular roads. The Spinney itself is a wood which was planted on a mound to commemorate the Heaton Pit Disaster in 1815 when 75 men and boys lost their lives. The pit closed in 1852 and 75 trees were planted on the site in memory of the lost men.

Many of the Victorian institutions had large tracts of land surrounding the premises. **Cherry Knowle Hospital** in Sunderland (NZ 401520) has vast grounds with plantations of trees and shrubs, mostly flanking internal roads. After the decline of country houses which began through the recession of the 1880s, hospitals and schools were often situated in converted estates. One example of this is at Dunston Hill, Gateshead, where the park has been preserved through institutional use of the buildings.

TEAM VALLEY TRADING ESTATE

The Team Valley Trading Estate, established in 1936, was one of the first purpose built industrial estates in the country. The 650 acre estate is recognised by Pevsner as a remarkable example of planned architecture by W Holford. The building of the estate involved extensive reclamation works and culverting of the River Team which originally was decorated with trellises and climbing roses. The estate was designed on a grid plan and consists of wide roads and verges. The double row of Wheatley Elm on Kingsway North is perhaps the most significant landscape feature. Originally, factories were encouraged to create their own garden areas, although sadly there are no remains. In the late 1980s the estate underwent a major environmental improvement scheme in an attempt to attract new development. This scheme by Brian Clouston & Partners reinforced many of the original features, including the replanting of the elm avenue with lime as well as solving unsightly late twentieth century problems such as the containment of car parking and storage yards.

RYHOPE PUMPING STATION — SUNDERLAND : NZ 403525

The pumping station was constructed from 1866 - 1870 by Sunderland and South Shields Water Company. Thomas Hawksley, an engineer of national fame, was commissioned to design the building and he adopted principles characteristic of such developments by using ornate architecture to conceal the industrial nature of the buildings. This approach was also reflected in the landscaping around the Italianate ponds. The site was densley planted with trees and shrubs and serpentine paths following routes around the ponds. Cleadon Water Pumping Station (NZ 389632) built c.1860, was also designed by Thomas Hawksley, again with careful landscaping of the site, and the mature trees are dominated by his towering chimney on the brow of the hill.

Ryhope Pumping Station, Sunderland.

CONTEMPORARY DESIGNED LANDSCAPES

Although the twentieth century does not feature strongly in this gazetteer, it is likely some contemporary landscapes will become tomorows' historic parks and gardens. Recent years have seen a dramatic greening of Tyne & Wear, through a wide range of reclamation and renewal schemes. Former coalfields and areas dominated by heavy industry have been revitalised to provide a more attractive environment for new industry, business, housing and retail development, as well as opening up large tracts of land for recreational and leisure uses. In particular the river corridors have been transformed by a number of projects by local authorities and more recently the Tyne & Wear Development Corporation.

The success of these projects is helping to stimulate a change in attitude towards the environment. As well as providing a place in which to work and rest and play it is also providing educational and cultural benefits; in many ways a return to the aspirations of Victorian park designers.

The 1960s and 1970s witnessed the start of large scale reclamation projects throughout the county. **Gateshead Riverside Park** marks a significant moment as it was one of the first reclamation schemes which was primarily a product of a landscape architect, Brian Clouston and Partners, rather than an engineer. The project went beyond the mere greening of a former spoil heap resulting in the existing mature rolling parkland which is particularly attractive when viewed from Newcastle and the river.

The Rising Sun Country Park, is North Tyneside's 400 acre green oasis but was formerly the site of the Rising Sun pit. It contains a Nature Reserve, Swallow Pond and a colliery subsidence pond formed around c.1935. The county's Nature Conservation Strategy includes many such sites and links them together along linear parks and wildlife corridors such as rivers, roads and railways, many of which have now become cycleways. Sunderland City Council and Tyne & Wear Development Corporation have initiated a number of linked landscape schemes which now form the River Wear Trail, including **Hylton Riverside Country Park** and the **Festival Park** adjacent to the Wearmouth Bridges near the city centre.

Large scale redevelopment programmes including the clearance of former terraces of housing continued through to the 1980s, for example at **Byker** which is described below. Here and in other housing developments large areas of designed green space were an essential component of the layout - no more so than at **Washington New Town** which consists of large areas of forestry planting composing a green grid within which villages and industry are located.

Environment has also become a useful marketing device and the inclusion of the word park has become a prerequisite for a desirable address - hence Business Park, Science Park, Technology Park, Enterprise Park and even Water Park. Of these Newcastle Business Park, landscaped by RPS Clouston, is a prime example of a successful reclamation and redevelopment scheme which as well as being a major business centre also contains a series of gardens and pieces of sculpture set within a fine new landscape adjacent to the Tyne.

What of the existing urban parks and gardens? There has been much debate recently on their current contribution and what their future role should be. Many are underused for a variety of reasons but there is enormous potential for renewal whilst respecting historical and cultural significance. An example of this is **Walker Park**, Newcastle upon Tyne, where new uses have been provided within a simplified layout. **Hodgkin Park**, Newcastle upon Tyne, is another Victorian park which is currently undergoing improvement works involving *artist in residence* Simon English.

BYKER — NEWCASTLE : NZ 270645

The Byker housing redevelopment scheme has won worldwide acclaim for it's innovative architecture and community based initiatives. Perhaps the most significant feature is the masterplanning and the successful integration of buildings and landscape by Ralph Erskine Architects and Landscape Architects. Byker marks the final phase of Newcastle City Council's massive slum clearance and redevelopment programme during the 1970s. The works began in 1971 and were completed in 1983. The terraced streets of Byker which formerly ran down the steep slope towards the river were replaced with a housing layout that exploited the south facing orientation towards the Tyne. A hierachy of external spaces has been devised, each with a particular function. Near the house, private gardens have been provided edged with low fencing and hedging. These look out onto a semi-private court, replacing the role of a terraced street but providing a safer place for children to play and an area for residents to adopt as their own. Beyond, the public realm includes a system of pedestrian links and larger open spaces including village greens and parks and areas of car parking. Throughout Byker natural materials have been used such as softwood timber, and stone and brick paving. In addition various salvaged architectural features have been incorporated. Planting is an essential component of the scheme, softening the impact of the high density layout, defining space and adding colour and vitality.

SEABURN PARK — CITY OF SUNDERLAND :NZ 40/54

Seaburn is the county's newest coastal resort and the *Lambton Worm* is the central piece of the childrens play area in the Worm Garden. This automated dragon sculpture with rolling eyes and water spilling out of it's mouth is a feature which recalls the joke *fountain trees* beloved of the Victorians which soaked unsupecting visitors.

PUBLIC ACCESS

HANGING GARDENS — NEWCASTLE : NZ 248636

This small park is located near the Redheugh Bridge, behind the recently completed Copthorne Hotel. The site had been derelict and neglected for many years until 1990 when it was reclaimed by the Tyne & Wear Development Corporation as part of the regeneration of the Quayside. The 1 in 1 gradient of the embankment presented a particular challenge to the designers, Anthony Walker & Partners, who incorporated a series of retaining walls, bridges, boardwalks, steps and ramps in order to provide public access and attractive sitting areas. Remains of Newcastle's town wall have been carefully integrated into the scheme. The project won the Landscape Institute's National Design Award in 1993.

PUBLIC ACCESS

illustration photo from Anthony Walker & Partners

NATIONAL GARDEN FESTIVAL — GATESHEAD : NZ 238617

National Garden Festivals were introduced by Michael Heseltine, then Minister for the Secretary of State for the Environment, as a means of urban regeneration. The basic objectives were to reclaim derelict land, to help improve image whilst providing a temporary tourist attraction and to offer an inviting site for subsequent development.

NGF '90 Gateshead was the fourth Garden Festival and the largest covering four linked areas and approximately 200 acres. One of the areas, Eslington Park, was earmarked by Gateshead MBC as a site for a permanent park. The area straddles the River Team and is bordered by high rise flats, a dual carriageway and a railway. The area designed by SGS Environment for NGF '90 includes significant mounding and strong blocks of planting within a design containing formal elements, including dramatic landscape features. The park has recently been further developed into a public park by Glen Kemp Hankinson for Gateshead MBC with the inclusion of recreational facilities and other features. Eslington Park won a Civic Trust Award in 1994.

PUBLIC ACCESS

National Garden Festival, Gateshead 1990.

CHIRTON DENE PARK, ROYAL QUAYS, NORTH SHIELDS : NZ 349675

Chirton Dene Park is a new 12 acre public park which opened in 1994. It is the primary open space within Royal Quays, Tyne and Wear Development Corporation's major regeneration scheme at North Shields. Formerly a dene infilled when the adjacent Albert Edward Dock was built in the 1880s, the area had been semi-derelict for many years. The park, designed by SGS Environment, includes water as the central theme, an element which in recent decades has largely been banished from public space. Water appears as a mountain stream, reed bed, central pool, a *chadar*, a boggy area for nature study and finally a series of dramatic cascades. The park's role in community development is illustrated by the play area which has been designed by Northern Freeform from local children's drawings and by the *Text Project* a collaboration of a local poet, Linda France and sculptor Alec Peever with local residents.

PUBLIC ACCESS

Cascades, Chirton Dene Park, North Shields.   *Royston Thomas (photo)*

SCULPTURE PARKS

Recent years have seen the artist play an increasing role in the design of landscapes. The greatest concentration of artworks in the area is found in the **Gateshead Riverside Sculpture Park** to the west of the Tyne Bridge. Perhaps the best known peice is *Rolling Moon*, by Colin Rose, with it's silver ball emerging above the trees as seen from the Metro and Newcastle Quayside. The park also boasts works by Richard Deacon, Maggie Howarth, Andy Goldsworthy, Richard Harris, Sally Matthews and a temporary piece by David Tremlett, with more installations expected! Other places where art is prominent in the county landscape include the work of Richard Cole at Windy Nook, near Felling, at North Shields Fish Quay, throughout the Great North Forest Area and at stations on the Metro, for example Raf Fulcher's garden at Jesmond where he created a sculpture *Garden Front* which originated from seventeenth century formal gardens with obelisks, topiary and grotesque arches.

Cone - Andy Goldsworthy

The Historic Parks and Gardens of Tyne and Wear : Index

Banqueting House
A building used as a room in the garden for eating and entertainment.

Bath house
A small building to shelter a cold bath.

Chadar
A water shute with a raised pattern which directs water to catch light as it falls.

Fernery
A collection of ferns, tender specimens being protected in a glasshouse and hardy species grown together outside as in a purpose built rockery screen as at Cragside, Northumberland.

Florist
A gardener besotted by a particular plant which was cultivated to perfect it's characteristics.

Gazebo
A pavillion of one or two stories used to view the garden.

Ha-ha
A sunken ditch, invisible from a short distance but restraining grazing animals from straying near the house.

Ice House
A deep pit built in shade or hillside, lined with brick or stone then packed with ice. Used for the preservation of food, meat in particular.

Knot garden
Continuous bands of low hedging forming symbolic knot patterns common in sixteenth and seventeenth century English gardens.

Orangery
As oranges were highly esteemed by gardeners but not hardy in our harsh climate it was necessary to cultivate the trees in a glasshouse.

Parterre
A terraced garden laid out with flower beds cut in elaborate patterns, to be viewed from above.

Pine Stove - Pinery
A greenhouse heated by stove for the cultivation of pineapples.

Pleasure Ground
A eighteenth century term for an area of lawn, ornamental planting and architecture to be viewed on foot.

Ride
A route, taken on horseback, enclosed by woodland along the edge of parkland, with intermittent views across the park.

Rond Pont
A circular area where avenues meet.

Rosary
A formal garden defined by arched trellis work. central circular trellises were also used to display roses.

Saltatorium - Deer Leap
A ditch by which deer could enter the deer park but not escape.

Topiary
trees trimed to geometric shapes such as cones or represdntational forms of creatures of objects.

Vinery
A glasshouse for cultivation of grapes, sometimes elaborate and used for entertainment.